THE PRACTICAL FLY FISHERMAN

THE
PRACTICAL
FLY
FISHERMAN

A. J. McClane

PRENTICE-HALL, INC., *Englewood Cliffs, New Jersey* 07632

The Practical Fly Fisherman by A. J. McClane
Copyright © 1975, 1953 by Prentice-Hall, Inc.
All rights reserved. No part of this book may be
reproduced in any form or by any means, except
for the inclusion of brief quotations in a review,
without permission in writing from the publisher.
Printed in the United States of America
Prentice-Hall International, Inc., London
Prentice-Hall of Australia, Pty. Ltd., Sydney
Prentice-Hall of Canada, Ltd., Toronto
Prentice-Hall of India Private Ltd., New Delhi
Prentice-Hall of Japan, Inc., Tokyo

10 9 8 7 6 5 4 3 2 1

Library of Congress Cataloging in Publication Data

McClane, Albert Jules.
    The practical fly fisherman.
    Includes index.
    1. Fly fishing. I. Title.
SH456.M15   1975   799.1'2   75-20383
ISBN 0-13-689398-8

ISBN 0-13-689380-5 {A REWARD BOOK : PBK.}

TO PAT

Come live with me and be my love,
And we will some new pleasures prove
Of golden sands and crystal brooks,
With silken lines and silver hooks.
John Donne

Foreword

by Arnold Gingrich

"I dreamed I was married to Al McClane," said my wife one morning recently, adding with a touch of asperity, "and you didn't seem to mind a bit."

"Maybe because I got custody of Patti and Susie on the exchange of punts," I suggested.

"Oh no. Patti flounced off in an Irish huff and Susie was already out somewhere with a horse. But you just stuck around and seemed to like it fine."

Well, it was a dream, and there's no accounting for them. But actually I welcomed the remark, because it furnished me a new way of saying that Al McClane is the one fisherman who in my eyes can do no wrong.

Hero worship exhausts all the superlatives after a while, so you welcome at all costs a new means of expressing how much you admire a guy. In *The Joys of Trout*, reaching for analogies, I'd already said that for me, just as there were no fiddlers beyond Kreisler and no tenors beyond Caruso, there were no fishermen beyond McClane. Fine. But what do you for an encore?

And what we have in hand here right now *is* an encore—a 1953 book, *The Practical Fly Fisherman*, back again by popular request after twenty-two years.

As it happens, my very next time at bat, in *The Fishing in Print* published in 1974, I touched on this volume in the course of harking back to a few fishing books that had been published anywhere from twenty-one to thirty-three years earlier, and had not only maintained their validity but even had it enhanced by comparison with some of the best books that have appeared only recently.

The point I was making was what a thrill it is when you pick up some old angling book and realize that it has foreshadowed discoveries that were made by others only much later on.

I cited several, and one of them was telling what a kick I got out of rereading Al McClane's chapter on "The Dry Fly Upstream and Down" in *The Practical Fly Fisherman*, at the very moment in the 1970s when the applause was still ringing in the rafters over the heterodox innovations of those Young Turks, Swisher and Richards, and the magician of the "sudden inch," the new master of the "worked" dry fly, Leonard Wright.

The citation wasn't meant to be mean, or to detract from the deserved success of the new young wizards (in fact I went on to join in the applause for them, because they're keeping things moving in the right direction toward experimental and innovative practices and avoidance of getting too set in any of the old ways), but rather it was meant to show how foresighted A. J. McClane was as far back as 1953.

I've been touting it, for that matter, from as far back as 1965, when I first listed it in *The Well-Tempered Angler* as one of the ten basic modern books, out of the thirty—classic, vintage, and modern—that I thought constituted a comprehensive course in angling literature, and entitled any man who read them all to regard himself as an educated angler.

It was then I found out, by what you may think is a pretty simplistic test, that this book, *The Practical Fly Fisherman*, had turned out to be the most useful—and living up to its name, the most practical—of all the fishing books I had. I'd long made a practice, with all angling books, of turning down the page corners whenever I came across something I hadn't read anywhere else, something I knew I'd want to come back to and make actual use of out on the stream. So one day, looking them all over, and their number was pretty high up in the hundreds at the time, I decided to see which one had the most page corners turned down. A lot of them had several—meaning anywhere between three and seven —but only one went beyond twenty. That was this one, which among all my books was and still is the undisputed champion with twenty-five. (The runner-up, in case you care, was *The Complete Fly Fisherman: The Notes and Letters of Theodore Gordon,* with nineteen).

Maybe you know a better way to judge the practicality of a fishing book, but I don't. I realize that practicality isn't the only test for the value and enjoyment of an angler's reading. By tradition angling books tend to be pretty discursive, and some, like Walton, you read not for practicality at all but rather, as Andrew Lang said, for "the perfume and the charm."

For all its high-practicality quotient, this book is pretty far out toward the middle of the mainstream of tradition in that respect too. It's by no means a mere manual. (Manuals are for mechanics, and properly shouldn't be counted as angling literature at all.) In his introductory chapter the author practically genuflects to the old established rule by promising that, once launched upon his discourse proper, we will "talk much and fish some." And he ends the introduction with a most seemly flourish. He ends it, in fact, with the most Waltonian sentence I can recall encountering anywhere outside of old Izaak's own pages: "May his days be blessed in sweet merriment." No anglers' prayer ever said it better.

But for all its engaging grace of presentation, this book never uses its genial rhetoric to paper over any gaps in the fundamental fact-structure of angling technique. It's all here—every least and last thing you have to know to undertake with success the actual angling that, in any event, only practice will gradually make more perfect. I say more perfect only because, despite the known longevity of fishermen, no angler will ever stay hale long enough to attain complete perfection.

The amazing thing is that the book is not dated, except for such self-evident differences as that fly lines float better now than they did in 1953, and are designated by numbers to indicate their weight instead of the old letters to indicate their diameter. Leader materials are also better now than they were then, and store-bought leaders are broader in butt and finer in tippet than they used to be. But you will find no better advice on how to proportion them for varying fishing needs and consequent variations of weight and length, than McClane gives you here.

Nor will you find, anywhere in print, any better account of how to perform the double-line haul than in the chapter "How to Cast Beyond Sixty Feet," and this despite the fact that in the intervening years everybody and his brother has had a crack at explaining it. The only difference time has made in that chapter is that Ellis Newman, who figures in it so prominently, is no longer around to demonstrate it, with or without a rod.

McClane's Standard Fishing Encyclopedia towers like a cathedral over the whole broad expanse of present-day American angling literature, of which it is by far the most imposing single structure. Next to it, of course, this little book is like a small cottage.

But it is big enough to hold everything you really need to be an angler. And as this present new edition after so much time attests, it was obviously built to endure.

Contents

THE PRACTICAL FLY FISHERMAN

Introduction

IT WAS the half-dark hour when nymphal garbs are shucked and delicate wings long dried in the sun pulsate in their first feeble movement. The river had given life to the plankton, and the plankton gave life to the nymph, and the dull, crisp shell of the nymph gave birth to the mayfly. She stepped lightly from the pondwort to feel the first strong flutter in her thinly veined wings; others came from the club moss, the fern, the woodbine, and the wild grape, all bearing a queer pattern of hallmarks—like fine etchings on their transparent wings. A gentle breeze blowing clean from the new mown hay brought heavy bodied land people tumbling through the air—the ants, the beetles, and the dark brown crickets. The clumsy caddis fly hung under his mottled roof-like wings, stumbling among the dancers with weighted feet.

The angler stood motionless in the river watching the mayflies whirl on a thin film of surface and, slowly at first, the trout appeared—a few scattered rises here and there. But soon, like dozens of slender fingers poised above the gravel, they gave the water life. This was the moment he had been waiting for; a great heavy-mouthed trout came out of hiding and drifted slowly to the center of the pool. His hand trembled slightly as the silk line rolled backward and forward. At the last turn forward he held his breath. The line pulled out straight and dropped softly to the river.

From somewhere deep in the chara weed the trout could see

1

a wavering, blurred image shifting on the surface; through lidless eyes it examined pinpoints of light made by the hackles—the same delicate impressions made by the legs of a mayfly. The fish slipped upward in a confident turn and sucked the fly under. In that instant the angler's wrist snapped backward and the fine wire barb held like a serpent's tooth. There was very little he could measure beyond the end of his rod tip—the length he had cast, perhaps—but not this first wild rush that quickened the imagination, the strong leap against dark willows when his eyes strained and his hand tightened, and the deep throbbing of the rod, pulsing with each twist of a heavy body. The trout bored down to the gravel to worry the fly, ripping bright yellow line from the angler's fingers. Suddenly the trout bolted away with the current and then up—up into the air, turning end over end. The play was over.

Lifting the great fish from the water, the angler held his net at arm's length. Did he see *a* trout, or *all* trout—the tired ones, the clowns, the acrobats, tight-skinned fish bursting with ova, slack-skinned fish dulled by winter currents, the hard-muscled ones who broke to freedom? Did he see a trout—an emotionless creature so removed in the chain of evolution that it carried the marks of age on its scales? Or did he see flaming gold and burnished silver, the deeper yellow of dust-coated fins, and the crimson spots—brilliant blood jewels of time, conceived in the womb of the river? For a moment he had halted life, to hold it in his net and wonder at its truth. A trout is not a snow covered mountain peak standing like a giant on the land for all to see. A mountain is a fact—a trout is a moment of beauty known only to men who seek them.

In his youth the angler had looked upon the face of the river and it revealed nothing; it was a blanket of glare without depth or meaning. Boy-like, he probed the surface with inquisitive casts, hour after hour, sometimes in a gray mist of wetness when black twigs spilled droplets on the earth. Sometimes under the intense blue of a summer sky when bleached rocks lay bare, sometimes he probed when red-brown leaves spiraled down and floated in heavy mats on the water. The boy cast to the boulders and searched the rapids, and the maiden fish and the kelt passed him by. He followed the shore and watched the currents, as millions had before him; the length of the river was out of the compass of his time, but her depth was the soul of all men born to angling.

And then one day he killed a trout, which he carefully washed clean and wrapped in ferns to bring to his father. The older man saw only a silent, glassy-eyed creature, so the boy scrubbed it all the harder, running cold water over the skin while telling of the flaming gold and burnished silver—but his treasures never came back. His father, wise in the ways of a fly-fisher, knew that the color was simply a pigment, a trick played by the chromatophores, and that his son saw a fragment of time which belonged to him alone. Perhaps this was what the angler remembered as he lowered the net and shook his trout free.

For two thousand years men have speculated on the ways of trout and their anglers, so when you begin the sport of fly-fishing it is important to know that there is much more here than meets the eye. To wear the clothing of an angler is not necessarily to be one, and the mere catching of fish is no recommendation to Walton's brotherhood of honest men. But this book is hardly a philosophy; I want to tell you something about fishing with artificial flies—and if in the course of it you discover that fly-fishing is as much a way of living as it is a method of angling, then so much the better.

The mechanics of fly-fishing are not difficult to learn, but it does take years of experience to become skilled in the game. There are sounds to interpret—the heavy sucking of brook trout feeding on the sedge, the delicate "pop" of a brown trout balanced in quiet water, and the explosions of salmon as they mount from the rapids. These are important and you will know them.

Trout have even been caught by faint changes in the wind—the pale breath of mint rising from springs, the firm colder draft of moving air set in motion by a rapid—these things tell us where gamefish hide.

Even time has a different meaning to the angler. There is a time for the mayfly hatch, a time for the caddis, a time to be on the river, and a time to be at a log fire. The angler does not ask time from a clock face. His time is in shadow and light—in dark forest of red-wood, the brightness of clear water, in the misty outline of a wet green meadow; his time is in sound—the rattling of insects on parchment wings; the toneless drumming of a partridge, the roaring sweep of a river beating against rock. His time is in silence—the dry silence of a canyon, the compelling silence of night—the silence of a billion leaves in summer and the tense silence of a coming storm. He stands apart from the precise steel mind of a clock when he wades to meet a river.

A man would look very foolish if he simply stood in the water without a rod and contemplated those sights and sounds known only to anglers. To justify his position, then, he carries the tools of angling. To lend authority to his search, the angler takes counsel of a fly box, wherein he stores his knowledge. From the dull feather of a partridge he can create the likeness of a stickleback; in the vibrant hairs of a bear he can imitate the flickering path of a humpback fry; from white strands of deer hair he paints the flash of a smelt. Like an artist working on good canvas, he measures the effect of each stroke against his hand. Thus, we have the "art" of fly-fishing to learn as well as the mechanics.

Our art has many branches, and a skilled angler will employ all of them. The dry or floating fly, the wet or sunken fly, bucktail and streamer, the nymph, and the bass bug—they all have a time and place. In the course of a day the weather may change. Winds can and do come up. Feed that was dormant a few hours earlier may become available, and even migratory game fish can appear. The shore line in fine detail is nothing but a series of casting problems, which can be attacked with varying degrees of success when using one method. And then we have the fish themselves—we are assuming that all our potential victims are of equal mind and appetite. This has never been a sound thesis when fishing big lakes; on a small mountain stream, perhaps, where any fly that sits on the water long enough to be seen will draw a trout from his hold. Food is hard to come by, and these fish will snatch things with no question of deceit. Even on larger rivers, trout may feed recklessly to a hatch of duns, and one can afford to be a purist.

For these and similar reasons, anglers are inclined to become a bit one-sided. In fact, we find specialists with specialties—fly fishermen who use nothing but dry flies to solve their private mysteries, wet fly fishermen who use nothing but a Royal Coachman in daylight and a Black Gnat after dark, and nymph fishermen who cast in no direction but upstream. Even in the narrow confines of their respective specialties, one specialist seldom agrees with another. Surely much good fishing is lost when the art is drawn so fine.

When we talk about fly-fishing, we're talking about many different kinds of fishing. The brown trout who pokes around the quiet waters of a Maine pond is only distantly related to the giant gravel knockers of a Utah river. And the brown trout of Pennsylvania, grown sharp in a mountain stream, is not the same fish as his namesake in a Scottish loch. Our fly fisherman would be technically hobbled if he couldn't produce a set of delicate dry flies to dance on the Schuylkill or a big Captain wet fly to swim in the Provo. It would be no less accurate to compare the kamloops rainbow of British Columbia to the coastal rainbows of Alaska—they neither look alike nor think alike. The fat brook trout of Manitoba, say one from the Nelson River, is many fishing practices removed from the tiny jewel found sculling in an Adirondack pond. The Alpine trout of England, the Arctic char of Greenland, and the *omble chevalier* of France are technically brothers, yet to catch one is no guarantee that you will catch the other.

As to bass, here one needs the wisdom of an Aristotle. The sleek smallmouth who drifts along limestone ledges in an Ozark stream is only distantly related to the shad-filled bruiser resting on the bottom of a Southern reservoir. A Florida largemouth grown mossy in a great sea of weeds is not the same bright bass you'll find in Lake Mead. It's a long way from the salt marshes of southern Virginia to a lake in Iowa, and the angler who takes largemouth bass in both is versatile indeed. This aside to you, good friend, in no way reflects the scope of this book so much as its limitations. I have fished in most places on several continents, but like any tourist with a collection of snapshots, I want to talk about the places I know best.

In this volume I have tried to demonstrate how you might put the smallest amount of study to best advantage. It follows that you will have to learn to cast well and gain a thorough understanding of what your tackle can and cannot do if you want to get the most out of a day on the stream. I don't pretend that the methods outlined in this book are perfect, but they represent what I consider a practical approach to fly-fishing. Of course, more than a thousand books were intended to expose the inner workings of a fish's mind, and this tome may resemble the others in setting and circumstance, but my words will not injure earlier authors because I am unable to report what a fish must think, and I submit that perhaps it doesn't matter. Few anglers are governed by what authors think—and least of all the authors themselves. Yet this confusion is productive of results as long as we remain within the limits of mutual experiences where bashful truths sit by the wayside.

And now it is time to get on with the angling. We shall talk much and fish some, and possibly our innocent design will compound a brew that will go off with an explosion, should we trap a reader who was unfamiliar with the ways of an angler. Perhaps he will regret his years spent away from rivers and now number his years in their wisdom. If so, let us fill our cup and drink to the coming fly-fisher. May his days be blessed in sweet merriment.

CHAPTER I

The Fly Rod

ANY NUMBER of skilled casters can throw a fly line beyond forty feet without using a rod. They just take a coil of line in one hand and a few extended feet in the other and begin casting. I can do it; the chances are you can too. Actually, casting without a rod isn't difficult if you have developed a sense of timing and a strong arm. It wouldn't be fun to fish this way, but hand casting begins to explain the role of a rod. Some people believe that the rod is more important to the angler than the line. Others say that it's the arm swinging the rod that decides a cast. And still others put the emphasis on the line and attach very little value to the rod. Obviously, if a man can cast long distances with nothing more than a line and his bare hands, then the most important elements of a cast are the work of his hands and the line itself. A rod therefore, is meant to simplify your hand movements in casting. When you buy a rod you must keep these questions in mind: How much effort must you apply to get the full lever length magnification of your wrist speed? Will the rod bend enough to compensate for awkward surges of speed? Does it have enough resistance to bend to accelerate the line automatically? Is the rod built to travel at identical speeds with the line?

It is surprising to learn how few fishermen are aware of the fact that a bamboo rod consists of a number of individual strips glued together. Many anglers with years of casting under their belts believe that a rod section is a solid piece of wood, bevelled along the edges to make it symmetrical. This is not possible with bamboo, as the raw cane is hollow, about two inches in diameter, and the inside surface is largely soft, pithy fiber. What we buy in a rod is for the most part the "skin" of the bamboo, plus some of the harder core lying underneath. Strip type construction also compensates for the grain structure characteristic of all natural rod building materials. To bend an ordinary square wooden timber with the grain is considerably easier than bending it at right angles to the grain. If we cut the beam in small strips, rearranging and glueing them together, we can even out some of these bending characteristics.

What, then, are the problems of a rod builder? First, he wants to build the rod of an efficient material, one that gives the angler a good return for the effort he expends in casting all day long; and secondly, he wants to distribute this material in the best possible manner, that is, give the rod an efficient shape. This shape is considered in two ways—the cross section of the rod, and its profile or taper. The material of which a rod is made determines what a rod will do, but the taper decides how that action will be controlled.

A fly rod has to bend and work equally well in any direction —up, down, sideways, across the flats or across the corners. You may think that only a round rod will bend in this way; so did the early rodmakers—they rounded off the corners of their rods, but this cut away the most valuable part of the bamboo. The idea of building rods of several strips of bamboo is quite old. They have been built from two to as many as twelve strips. For one reason or other, most of these rods had an even number of sides—four, six, eight, and so on. But the odd angles didn't get much attention until Robert W. Crompton of St. Paul, Minnesota, analyzed the situation and concluded that the five-strip construction was superior in nearly every respect. Crompton laboriously planed a set of sticks by hand, following the taper of his favorite six-strip rod. Finally it was finished. Trial proved the new five-strip rod much too stiff. Both rods had the same amount of wood, the very same taper, but the pentagonal type

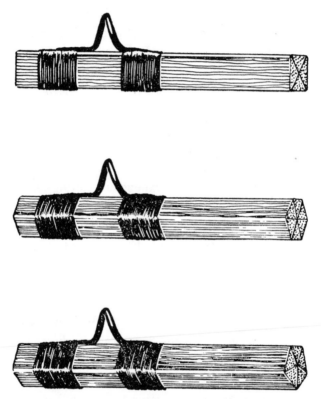

Figure 1. *According to the five-strip theorists, the four-strip rod* (top) *is more flexible in the plane of its corners, the six-strip rod* (center) *is more flexible in the plane of its flats, while rods of pentagonal construction* (bottom) *are more flexible in a plane slightly to the side of each corner.*

felt, as he expected, much stiffer. A great deal of interest was aroused when this fact was brought to the attention of his rod-building friends, Dr. George Parker Holden and Perry Frazier, but finding the right tapers for this construction was to evolve over a period of fifty years. He pointed out the five-strip's merits; no continuous glue line through the center as in even-sided rods. The shearing stress or working strains were borne by the bamboo fiber. Then there was about 15 per cent less glue. He pointed out that if a rod were made of a great number of strips, it would consist principally of glue, and glue is no substitute for bamboo. He explained the unusual stiffness by sketching a pentagon—the cross section of a five-strip rod—pointing out the fact that the five corners were opposed by flat sides. These corners were in effect, little backbones that ran the entire length of the rod.

It's this "backbone" theory that caused conventional rod makers to pop their buttons, and at the same time brought five-strip adherents into a common bond of understanding. But before the argument against, let's examine the case for the five-strip idea more closely. The leading modern exponent of pentagonal construction is Nat Uslan of Spring Valley, New York. Nat is an old friend of the late Robert Crompton, a master rod builder, and by far one of the keenest artisans in his trade. In the Uslan school of design, the argument against even-sided construction is that corners are opposite corners and flats are opposite flats. The corners, in the five-strip rod, act as backbones extending the length of the rod, but in four- and six-strip rods they are in the same plane—that is, directly opposite each other. Since there are three pairs of flats, it follows that the action, or bending, will occur in one or more of these three planes. In theory, if the fisherman forces a corner to take some of the load, it simply "shrugs" the load over to one of the adjacent flat sides, with the result that the cast doesn't go exactly where he directs it. This is an inherent characteristic of all rods having an even number of sides according to the pentagonal theorists.

A five-strip rod doesn't respond in such a manner. In this case each "weak" flat has a reinforcing backbone on the opposite side.

Naturally, the strengthening is greatest right at the five corners. At points slightly to one side or the other of these corners the effect diminishes slightly only to increase again to full value as the center of the bordering flat side (remember that there is a corner opposite this flat) is reached. A four-sided rod prefers to bend up and down and sideways. To use shooters' parlance, it wants to swing directly from twelve to six o'clock or from three to nine, but it resists bending slightly more in any other combination. By the same reasoning a rod of six-strip construction will flex easily from twelve to six, from two to eight, and from four to ten. It, too, is reluctant to bend in any other direction. The five-strip rod is no exception to this tendency to follow paths of least resistance. But where are these paths and how many of them are there? According to Nat Uslan they're not at corners because these regions are strongest; nor are they at the flats because, as pointed out before, there is always a corner opposite a flat. Then these "flexing planes" must necessarily lie somewhere between a corner and the next flat. Since there are ten such combinations of corners and flats, we can assume that the five-strip rod doesn't care which way you shoot your cast. This is the essence of pentagonal design, and right or wrong, there's no question but that Nat Uslan makes a fine fly rod.

The six-strip or hexagonal fly rod is the traditional construction among rod builders the world over. Ever since a gunsmith by the name of Samuel Phillippe, of Easton, Pennsylvania, began playing with bamboo strips back in 1845, speculative rod makers have championed every possibility, from two strips to twelve. But Mr. Phillippe's six-strip rod caught on, and it remains today as the *crème de la crème* of even-sided building. Now the proponents of Phillippe's school have some sound arguments against five-strip theory, and the two things they talk about in comparing the five and the six are weight and stiffness. The weight depends on the area of the cross-section, so when you compare cross-sections of these two rods you are really comparing the weights of the five and the six. So if the two cross-sections are of the same area, this indicates the same weight. The other factor, stiffness, is measured by what an engineer calls the "moment of inertia" of a cross-section. (The moment of inertia of a circular cross-section varies as D^4, or the diameter to the fourth power. Thus a circle one inch in diameter is $1 \times 1 \times 1 \times 1 = 1$. A circle 1.1 inch in diameter is $1.1 \times 1.1 \times 1.1 \times 1.1 = 1.45$, or almost 50 per cent stiffer.)

This is the point on which rod builders of the two schools really disagree. The fact is that if the cross-section is made up of any number of equal triangles with their inner points on a common center, their outer points on one circle and their outer flats on another circle—the rod will be equally stiff in every direction. And that holds true whether the cross-section is a triangle, a square, a pentagon, a hexagon, a septagon, an octagon, or in fact a figure with an infinite number of sides—a circle.

All fishing rods which have guides and reel attached tend to cast in a preferred plane, because the center of gravity of the whole outfit is offset from the center axis. If you bend a piece of hexagonal split cane in your hands, it will feel stiffer bent across corners, because the pressure applied to your hands, in pounds per square inch, by a corner is greater than that applied by a flat. You get exactly the same false impression by bending five-strip "flat-up" and "flat-down"; the latter feels softer.

Any construction consisting of a regular polygonal cross-section having four or more sides will have the same deflection for a given load irrespective of the plane in which it is bent, whether across corners or across flats. Richard Walker, well known British angling writer, even took this problem to Cambridge University to get a precise, mathematical explanation, and this is what he concluded in a recent letter to me:

The rigidity of a rod depends on the moment of inertia of its cross-section, and the values for various constructions are as follows:

Maximum stress for bending moment (M)		Radius of Circumscribing Circle	Moment of Inertia (I)	
4-strip	.812 a/4	1.252a	M/a-3	1.54
5-strip	.795 a/4	1.15 a	"	1.45
6-strip	.791 a/4	1.10 a	"	1.39
7-strip	.787 a/4	1.073a	"	1.363
circle	.786 a/4	a	"	1.274

Where "a" equals the radius of a circle of equal cross-sectional area to each of the polygons, I give the radius of the circumscribing circle of each polygon in terms of "a," and also the maximum stress; this might be described as the "likelihood of breakage" index. You will observe that the change in rigidity from 5-strip to 6-strip is insignificant and is offset by the change in the maximum stress figure.

Having come thus far in this mathematical orgy, you may be disturbed by my clinical treatment of this precious thing called a fly rod. No doubt you care not a fig for analysis, so long as the rod gives you pleasure. But before we can set forth in straight-forward speculation about fishes and their ways, we must first see to our tools in order that we are not left in the frivolous ranks of gullible anglers. Our rod engineers are arguing, and now, to some extent we know what they are arguing about. At this point I would like to offer my own opinion and say that I own four-strip, five-, six-, and seven-strip rods, and all but the seven-strip construction is good. I think all these didactic discussions have no future because the most important ingredient of a rod, and one which is never discussed, is its taper. In finding the perfect rod with any kind of cross-section one must find the perfect rod for that *length*. This is purely a rod builder's problem, and one in which we won't get lost. Let's offer this thesis to posterity so that when historians dig among our ruins a hundred years hence they will find some kernel of controversy which they cannot disprove. So now we'll look at other forms of construction, ignoring the strips and considering the material.

In this search for greater rod power at any given rod weight, Lew Stoner of the Winston Rod Company in San Francisco evolved the fluted hollow construction. Working under the assumption that a tube is the strongest form which can be given to any cross-section of any material, Lew decided that here was the answer to the perpetual challenge to rod makers—to use a structure which would come within the $5\frac{3}{4}$-ounce weight limit applied to tournament rods at one time, having the greatest power potential. For over thirty years the distance limit of tournament casting had been between 130 and 140 feet; but rod makers knew that the range could be extended if they found a way of making a stronger rod. The British steel centered rod was strong, but far too heavy. The double-built cane rod was even better for casting, but this too was heavy. If live bamboo could grow under the winds of a tropical typhoon, Lew assumed that its natural hollow form was proper for a fishing rod. But to get greater strength and widen the surface of the glue seam he arched the interior of a hexagonal rod, rather than just circling out a hollow. This fluting made the cane more resistant to external crushing and provided the needed surfaces to secure the splines. His first rod was $\frac{5}{8}$-inch thick at the hand grasp, $\frac{11}{32}$-inch at the ferrule, and $\frac{1}{8}$-inch thick at the tip-top, and although it was 10-feet long the rod weighed $5\frac{3}{4}$-ounces. The rod was hollow, nearly all of the soft pithy fiber was removed, and nothing but the hard outer shell of bamboo remained.

This rod at once set new world casting records of over 160 feet in the hands of Marvin Hedge and G. L. McLeod in 1938. The next year Dick Miller sent the record up to 183-feet, 3-inches with another Winston rod. Although this has been exceeded in practice casts, it hasn't been beaten since in tournaments. But the fluted hollow construction made one factor obvious, that weight was no longer a criterion for rod power, either in a tournament rod or a fishing rod. Thus, the fluted hollow school came into being. The word "power," incidentally, is more correctly defined as the ratio of weight to elasticity in a rod sense, and is reflected in the speed of that rod. We are not talking about springs and things that jump in the air. The next landmark in the search for greater rod power concerned an entirely new material—fiberglass. Dr. Arthur M. Howald introduced the first glass rod in 1946, and it's perfectly obvious that this has been the greatest development in rod building in the past fifty years.

When glass rods first appeared on the market they were expensive and had poor action. But glass could take far more abuse than bamboo; it had a much higher breaking point and could be bent into fantastic shapes. One of the more popular demonstrations at the sport shows had a salesman pulling his customer across the floor while the prospective buyer was seated on a chair. This was usually done with a bait casting rod and heavy line, and it made a great impression. The strength of glass was undeniable, but the bugbear that bothered critical casters was the rod's performance. Some of these fly rods vibrated so much that they threw humps in the line, and none of them had the delicate feel of a bamboo rod. Today glass still doesn't have quite the delicate response of cane, but a glass rod with the proper action will match or excel the performance of many bamboo rods on the present market. I like glass fly rods for heavy fishing—bass bugging, steelhead fishing, and salt water fly fishing—where a fine sense of touch is unimportant. Because of its high tensile and compressive strengths, elasticity, and infinite fatigue life, this material is ideally suited to any casting that exposes the rod to knocks, bumps, sudden stresses and prolonged strain.

The name "glass" is misleading when used in reference to

rods. A good many people think of a transparent, unbendable, easily broken window pane, and wonder how the stuff can be melted into a rod. The difference lies in fibers; fine glass fibers look and feel like silk, and the smaller ones that go into some rods are so thin that they're almost invisible. These fibers come from carefully tested raw materials, and are literally drawn from molten glass marbles. To get these fine strands into a rod form, they are treated chemically and then held together with a resin or plastic bonding agent.

The glass content of fishing rods, for instance, ranges from as little as 35 per cent to as much as 75 per cent, according to the type and quality of the rod. The smaller the diameter of the shaft, the greater the percentage of glass necessary to give backbone to the rod. Naturally, the degree of flexibility decreases as the percentage of glass increases, so it is a matter of arriving at the correct formula in which the proper blending of glass content with resin, coupled with the correct tapering, results in the best rod.

Although a solid glass rod is stronger than hollow glass, by the same token, it is heavier. In fly-fishing, rod weight is a deciding factor, and consequently all our glass fly rods are hollow or else the glass fiber cloth is wrapped around a core made of some light weight material. The strength and action of a hollow glass rod are dependent upon such factors as the number of layers of cloth, thickness of the cloth, lamination of the wrap, length of the rod itself, and the degree of mandrel taper. Each manufacturer endeavors to develop a mandrel which is in his opinion what the market requires. The process of making a hollow glass rod is to roll the fiber glass cloth tightly in layers on a steel mandrel having the exact tapered dimension required for the rod being manufactured. The number of layers and the thickness of the cloth will vary with the type of rod being made. After it has been rolled, the wrapped mandrel is placed in an oven where the glass cloth layers and strands are bound together by the hardening or "curing" of the resin. Following this baking cycle, the mandrel is withdrawn and the resulting hollow blank is sanded or rubbed smooth, and finished with coats of varnish, lacquer, or resin, in accordance with the practice of the individual manufacturer. The butt, guides, and reel seat are then assembled to finish the rod.

The fly rod market today is fast resolving itself to the mass produced glass rod and the custom tailored bamboo rod. The glass houses of angling, South Bend, Shakespeare, Heddon, Narmco, Harnell, Montague, Horrocks-Ibbotson, and many others are turning out fine rods at low cost. In fact the industry reports that fifteen million have been sold in the past seven years and there's no denying the fact that Fiberglas is going to dissolve all the pleasant arguments we had about cross-sections of cane. Perhaps the ratio of glass to plastic will serve as well. But the connoisseur of fine rods is still going to go to men like Lew Stoner, E. C. Powell, Everett Garrison, Nat Uslan, Wes Jordan, Pinky Gillum, Bill Taylor, Jim Payne, and the Edwards brothers to buy those precise instruments that are born in a small workshop even if he has a closet full of glass rods. If the superiority of glass rests on a showdown between strength and beauty, we had better take pause. Bamboo is not a material that can be made from a synthetic cloth by white coated women working with conveyor belt efficiency. Does glass have the warm affection of an Everett Garrison? Or the patient care of a Jim Payne? This is a point of economic philosophy, and the reader must resolve the contents of his own closet if this chapter is to remain objective.

Fly rods are usually identified as being a wet fly action, dry fly or trout action, bass-steelhead action, and salmon action. These terms are descriptive enough for the novice, but more precise information is desirable for the advanced angler as some of these terms are interchangeable. A dry fly "action" is quite suitable for wet fly fishing, and a high quality wet fly action often makes a perfect dry fly rod. For salmon fishing I would never use anything heavier than a bass-steelhead action, and the rod I like best for salmon is a light dry fly action. If we dig a bit deeper we find that the wet fly rod is a lighter rod at any given length than a comparable dry fly rod. Rods for the wet fly are soft, as there is little false casting to be done. A stiffer rod would dry the fly while false casting and is therefore less desirable. So the dry fly rod is comparatively stiff and has a more pronounced tip movement, a quality that is built into the rod rather than added to it by an increase in weight. Bass-steelhead rods are heavier and stiffer because the flies and lures used for these fish are heavier and more wind resistant. Essentially they are slow but powerful. Salmon action rods are the heaviest and stiffest by far, because of the weight of line and the size of the flies these rods must throw. But if the fisherman chooses to ignore the traditional double hook salmon flies and has the skill to lay out a long line with a light rod—any of the other rods can be used. These terms then, are simply a guide for the beginner.

Robert W. Crompton once paid a college professor to work out a taper for the stiffest rod for its weight. The finished design had a broad base and a slim top, very much like the design of the Eiffel Tower. But the completed rod was limber instead of stiff and unsatisfactory as a fishing rod. The reason Crompton's professor failed was because he assumed that a rod is a cantilever beam—which it is until you pick it up and begin casting—then you have a simple beam with cantilevers at both ends. The rod is immediately divorced from the classic field of static mechanics and becomes a subject of dynamics; it acquires properties of acceleration, impact, rotation, momentum, and a host of others. Once the rod has motion there are two supports—the hand which is supporting the butt, and the nodal point in the tip. This nodal point is the area of transition where the force applied to the butt of the rod is being translated into motion.

My rod building friend, Alan Palmer, demonstrates this by

holding a fly rod a few inches over and parallel to the floor. When he raises the rod sharply to flip the tip upward, the butt part of the rod comes up with his hand but the tip moves in the opposite direction, striking the floor before rebounding and following the direction taken by the butt. I wouldn't suggest that you bang a good fly rod on the floor, but the fact remains that you can't give a fly rod casting impetus and get a single response. You can get the idea by holding your rod horizontally and setting up a side to side vibration with your wrist. As the tip fans out, notice the nodal point—the upper third of the rod continues to bend in a direction opposite to the movement of your hand for just a fraction of a second before rebounding to catch up with your wrist speed.

So now we can begin to see what rod action is. The best definition I have ever heard is Alan's, and this is the way he describes it: "A rod can be broken down into three convenient and easily recognized sections, the tip, middle, and butt. In actual casting the hand drives the butt, the butt drives the middle, and the middle drives the tip, and, of course, the tip drives the line. The tightness or looseness of this linkage is the action of a rod." So, the action is controlled largely by the stiffness of the middle portion. The butt is the driver, the tip its translator, and the midsection and arched truss between the two. When a fish is hooked, the rod once again becomes a static cantilever beam with certain bends and hollows—an uneven elastic arc.

Obviously then, this linkage must have a smooth harmony. If the rod tip is too fine or too weak, it will vibrate badly, or when full power is applied, it will bend excessively, breaking up the rod curve and progressiveness of power. The stiff butt of tip action rods stops the action too high, also breaking up the progressive-uniform curve of rod. This must be compensated by extra forearm and wrist power, which destroys the harmony between tip and butt. With a tip-heavy rod you cannot make the fly travel slowly from rear to front, for the heavy tip gives too much speed to the line with a jerky motion. You have to give it short, fast strokes, thus eliminating all possibilities of progressive power. On short casts there is no fine feeling of "tip in hand," and it is very tiring on your wrist.

Many rods made in the United States back in the 30's had butts that were much too soft, giving them a "hammer," tip-heavy action, as the tip was too heavy for the butt. The ideal rod action should and can perform like this: Always have the tip-in-hand feeling; give perfect casts with greatest ease, using only wrist and other parts of arm when desired; at all distances the action should be complete. You can have an ideal short and medium range fly rod with all the power reserve for exceptionally long casts, without losing any of the qualities of light tip action and English type soft action rods. Maximum casting power with minimum muscle power, perfect side cast, perfect left and right side casts, perfect overhead casts, perfect sky casts, perfect roll casts. No line hump. Cast a wide or narrow loop—and remain smooth at all times. It should be a perfect wet and dry fly. And in my opinion, the length should be at least 8½ feet if you are only going to work with one rod.

There are many ways of selecting the right dimensions for a rod that will suit your particular fishing. You might decide upon a short rod, for instance, if most of your casting is on small streams where brush and overhanging limbs interfere. Or you might want a long fly rod to make casting from a boat or canoe easier; the longer rod would have better control over the line and it would toss the fly to much greater distances. But other people will point out that a short rod offers better leverage against the fish, and if properly made it will cast fishable distance with much less effort. The long rod man will counter this by saying that because of better line control he can cast on any small stream within reason, and he still has the advantage of greater range. Inasmuch as our general concept of short and long is a 7½-foot rod on one hand, and an 8½-foot rod on the other, it's hard to accept the fact that a one foot difference in length is going to make brush casting easier. Having owned rods of every description that swished and swashed through hours of casting, I am completely sold on the long rod for all types of fishing. So, for the novice starting out with one rod, I'd recommend an 8½-foot, dry fly action, which in a top quality grade should weigh about 5 ounces, and in less expensive makes about 5½ ounces.

Describing fly rods by weight, in an effort to describe rod power, is confusing and difficult. For the lack of anything better this system has been used by manufacturers and anglers for years, but I seriously doubt if a more practical solution will be found. A 5½-ounce tournament distance rod has almost unbelievable power. It's stiff, heavy, and you couldn't fish with it for more than a few minutes. Practically all the weight is in bamboo; there will be a minimum of light wire guides, little or no reel seat, and just enough cork on the grip to keep your hand from cramping. The ferrule will be made of a very light metal. When compared to a standard 5½-ounce fishing rod with a comfortable cork handle and screw locking reel seat, you realize immediately the latitude that exists within 5½-ounce types. These same differences exist to a lesser degree between all standard rods, but for critical fishing they are important.

For purposes of discussion, let's consider the glued-up cane of our 8½-foot rod—the six strips cemented and ready for mounting. Now assume that we have two such canes made by two different builders and the sticks are absolutely identical. They are not yet rods. To become rods they will have to have reel seats, hand grasps, guides, ferrules, and a good varnish job. Reel seats have been made that weigh as little as ½-ounce, and many of them weigh 1½-ounces, so our two builders could conceivably start off with an ounce and a quarter difference in one item alone. Ferrules can be of several metals, many thicknesses, and a number of lengths. Even identically-sized ones can vary in weight, and one builder may use two ferrules on his 8½-foot rod, while the other will use only one. In hand grasps, even the cork will vary greatly in weight. A dozen cork rings can add an eighth of an ounce more than another dozen taken from the same lot. And when it comes to the diameter of the grip, you would be amazed at the difference in weight between one size or shape and another. The number of guides which serve to hold the line to the rod and distribute strain when the rod is under stress will be at least nine and possibly eleven. When our two builders finally varnish their rods there will not only be another increment in weight to consider but possibly a difference in action. A soft varnish makes a soft rod, and it will kill its resiliency if too much is used.

Remember, in our original premise we assumed two identically made canes. We didn't even consider the fluted hollow construction of Lew Stoner, or the impregnation process used by Wes Jordan at Orvis; either one would add considerable power and variations in weight to our hypothetical 8½-foot rod. We didn't consider glass, beryllium, copper, or steel, and we didn't allow for the variations in bamboo itself. There are many varieties of bamboo, all of them differing in specific gravity. Rods made from large butt cuts will be heavier, though much superior in casting qualities to those made from top cuts or smaller diametered canes. Other performance factors are perfections and imperfections in cutting and gluing the splines, the seasoning of both the raw bamboo and the glued-up canes, and the type of glue and varnish used. So now you might realize that two "identical" 8½-foot rods can differ by at least one ounce and have entirely different actions. One maker may aim for lightness, and the other for purpose. When you go into a rod shop and ask for an 8½-foot, 5½-ounce rod, the man behind the counter will probably have a dozen of them but only a few will fit your requirements. They might range from powerful steelhead rods to light dry fly rods, and with nothing more in mind than a weight specification you might be handed any one.

Few people can explain how a television set works, why a doorbell rings, or how that mechanical monster the refrigerator makes little ice cubes. Yet tiny tots can turn these things on and off, and as they get older they even learn which of these indigestible miracles is working properly. Fly rod action is less comprehensible than a plague of locusts or surrealistic art, but since it is a functional tool like the refrigerator you soon learn whether the darn thing is producing or not. Through my magazine and newspaper columns in the past seven years, I have recommended an 8½-foot, 5½-ounce fly rod to thousands of novice anglers. A good many of these people wrote back a year or so later to tell me how they progressed, and in view of their pleasure, it appears that a rod approximating these dimensions is as near to an all-purpose tool as one can get. It has the spirit to throw small bass bugs but just enough delicacy to make nice casts with the dry and wet fly. For streamer flies and bucktails it's a bit shorter than I would like my rod to be, and for the wear and tear of spinner fishing it's a bit light. But we can't have everything in one rod. Later you can buy a proper dry fly rod, a heavier one for bass bugging, and maybe a long soft rod just for wet fly fishing. Just don't make the mistake of buying a light rod for light fish, and a heavy rod for heavier fish. The fly rod must fit the job. General Lindemann tells a story about angling in Scotland which explains this point more graphically.

It seems that Lord Trippingham went one holiday to the Dee River, a stream that is bathed in the finer distinctions between tackle and anglers. To Trippingham was appointed a dour Scot gillie who obviously didn't approve of his 12-foot, 16-ounce salmon rod—an appalling weapon, even on the mighty Dee. It was an affront to Sandy's profession having to guide a gentleman who would use such heavy tackle. They passed a silent morning until they reached a grand pool below the village of Aberdeen.

After awhile, Trippingham hooked something heavy. He played his quarry for an hour in strong currents, and when the old boy was tuckered out, he called for the gaff. Sandy peered over the bank and then, with a deft stroke of his iron, he beached a very waterlogged corpse. Trippingham was at once thunderstruck: "By Jove, what a catch!" Sandy regarded the corpse rather disdainfully and said: " 'T isn't much sir, 't was only the postmistress, she barely weighed a hunret pounds."

Although fiberglass was a relatively new rod material when I wrote this chapter, it deservedly captured the mass market. But as I anticipated, bamboo still has a faithful following among freshwater anglers. Prices have risen to astronomical heights. To buy a Garrison, Gillum, Payne, Powell, Leonard, Thomas, Young, or any of the classics is investing in art—not simply from the aesthetic view but also in terms of resale value. Not long ago a secondhand bamboo rod would fetch a few dollars; now prices are double and triple the original cost. The great craftsmen were quality-oriented. I own a Paul Young Perfectionist, for example, which is entering its twenty-fifth season, and except for having it refinished once before Paul died, the rod is as good as new. The little stick has stood the test of time and several large Atlantic salmon.

Fiberglass has been a real boon to saltwater angling and here it dominates the field. The abuse and stresses of marine fly fishing have no counterpart in freshwater. Inevitably rods get knocked about in small skiffs for a variety of reasons and the sheer weight of many saltwater gamefish which must be snubbed at boatside or pumped from deep water puts a premium on the strength of a shaft rather than its casting qualities. There is nothing delicate about a tarpon, bonefish, permit, or striped bass, and even the act of striking requires considerable force to set the hook. I use a bamboo rod on rare occasions when conditions are optimum, such as wading a flat for small fish as opposed to casting from a skiff; but cane has virtually disappeared from the saltwater scene.

There are recently developed rod-building materials, notably boron and high-modulus graphite (1973). I believe the latter will replace fiberglass during the next decade. Graphite is not only lighter by 25 to 30 percent at any equivalent work load, but has double the mechanical strength. A graphite rod can pick up long lengths of line with little effort on the angler's part, and it can be fished all day long without wrist fatigue.

CHAPTER II

How to Cast

WHENEVER I think of fly casting, I remember a July afternoon in France, when Charles Ritz demonstrated what can be accomplished after a lifetime of angling. The Risle is a beautiful river throughout its length. It meanders between gentle hills, touching the feet of ancient Norman castles. Crossing farmlands, it reaches thick stands of poplar and willow before a long run to the North Sea. The name "chalk stream" is derived from the calcareous clay bottom, typical of those streams that were part of the ocean centuries ago.

The trout that live in these waters offer a sport that cannot be paralleled by any other type of fishing. They are wise to the point of distinction, they feed in the most impossible places—in pockets as big as a teacup, and channels no wider than this page —and they can make the most expert angler look, feel, and act awkward. A close approach is impossible, and drag on the line is a certainty because of the necessity for cross-stream casts. In short, it is the finest school in the world for a dry-fly angler. There is no protective current or cover to screen the angler's errors.

The stretch we were looking at was a long piece of crystal-clear water bordered by tules, barbed wire and sun-bleached cows. It was like many other sections of the river, but with one important difference—the weeds did not grow to the surface. There were fully two feet of open water above the swaying vegetation; from bank to bank it was a smooth run. Several large trout were feeding in midstream. Telltale bubbles floated down, following the soft, dignified suck of trout that would heft two pounds or more.

The trout that Charley wanted was a steady feeder, a methodical food collector who loafed just under the surface in the shadow of a willow sweeper on the far side of the river. This was an impossible cast. The trout was fully eighty feet away and holding in such a position that the leader would have to fall completely to the left, if the fly were to reach under the branches and cover the fish. In effect, it was like casting around a corner. We crouched in the grass and watched the big brownie tipping up and down, taking every bug that came along. Charley rose cautiously, rod cocked, and with all his line coiled carefully at his feet. When it comes to the smooth beauty of effortless fly casting, he is a master. The yellow line flicked skyward in the blink of an eye, lengthening in fast pulls as he extended about fifty feet in an upstream direction. In the clear, shadowless waters of a chalk stream even the motion of a high flying line might easily send the fish running for cover, so Charley made his false casts well out of the fish's sight.

Not only was the cast directed away from the trout, but because of the angle he now needed twenty or twenty-five feet more to reach the other bank. Charley made very few false casts actually, and when his rod had reached pulling load, he leaned hard against the bamboo and with a quick shift of his wrist sent the line speeding across stream where it was checked hard just below the target. The leader turned gracefully to the left, propelling the little brown bivisible below the willows. The fly was sucked under in a tiny bubble, through the deliberate, slow rise of a completely duped trout. Of forty yards of fly line, only the last few inches hung in the rod guides when the trout came up. That was one of the greatest fishing casts I have ever witnessed.

I have fished with some of the world's finest casters, Tommy Edwards, Pierre Cresevaut, Charley Ritz, Bedell Smith, the late

Art Neu, and others whose rod work is almost legend. At first glance, there's a definite pace in the motions of all of them; the fly flicks out, drifts back, is lifted and recast—out and back again, a thousand times. The angler steps forward, perhaps to change his line of drift or cover another fish—the fly flicks out, drifts back and suddenly disappears in a swirl. But after careful study, the fact most apparent is that there can't be *one* correct style. The positions from which talented casters work smoothly and accurately are numerous. They all move their rods in a plane suited to the individual cast and are rarely in the classic pose. Accuracy, distance, and delivery are the result of long familiarity with tackle; they are not a gift or an accident.

The best any book on fly casting can hope to achieve is to make certain elementary steps clear. Even this is a considerable undertaking because there are often two ways of doing the same thing. I will describe what I think is the easiest method, or at least the one that will be most profitable to you, and in later chapters we can examine other possibilities.

So, with the rod set up, the reel underneath, grip the cork firmly in your right hand—with your thumb extending along the top. If you're a southpaw, do exactly the same thing with your left hand. Either way, the hand you cast with is your *rod hand*. To be clear, the instructions following will be for right-handed casters. First, get out about two rod lengths of line to provide enough weight to begin. Do this by pulling it off the reel with your left, or *line hand*, and switch the rod back and forth. Now, to start a cast, lift the rod back smartly until it is vertical. Do not bring it back any further; that is one of the commonest faults of a beginning caster. The bending of the rod and your wrist speed will send the line into the air in back of you. This is called the *back cast*. When the line has straightened out in the rear—and not until then—bring the rod forward just far enough to get maximum line speed again. Both these motions, back and forward, must be blended together smoothly, yet with emphasis.

As the line shoots forward, it gradually unrolls until the leader straightens out and the fly drops to the water.

To digress for a moment, if the line is properly cast, it does not go through the air on a plane parallel with the water. On the back cast, the end of the line must be above your head, and on the forward cast it should finish below your head. If you allow the rod to go beyond the vertical on the back cast, the

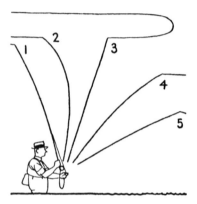

Figure 2. *A good forward cast is blended with the back cast. At position 1, the angler has completed his back cast, letting his line straighten in the rear. Then, applying power from positions 2 to 3, he follows through to 4, the rod drifting down to 5 as the unrolling line loses its momentum.*

line will fall too far below in the rear and be too high on the forward cast. These casting planes can be altered for distance casting or special casts, but concentrate first on fundamental movements. If you have gripped the rod properly, you will find that your wrist is blocked when the rod reaches the perpendicular. The line will fall low in the rear if you raise your forearm, so be careful to emphasize the wrist movements in order to make the rod work.

It takes just as much power to throw the line 40 feet behind you as it does to make a forward cast of 40 feet. Watch your back cast for a while and keep it high. Apply enough power so that the line straightens out, and begin the forward cast when it is extended or nearly so. It is all right to let the rod drop back slightly after the back cast has been completed. This will leave you in a better position to start the forward cast.

On the river you can follow this procedure exactly, except that you will make several casts in the air. These are called false casts. False casting serves to dry the fly out in case you are dry fly fishing, and also creates greater line speed, so that you can extend or shoot your fly to greater distances. The final forward cast should be aimed at a spot from two to three feet over your target, and the cast is checked slightly when the line straightens to cause your fly to drop softly and naturally. Correct presentation of the fly is assured by stopping the rod tip a little high on the forward cast so the fly is cast over, and not on the water. Aim at a place above or beyond the spot where you want to place the fly, and as the leader turns over, release line, letting a few inches out. This absorbs the power of the cast, and the fly will almost stop in the air. There are other ways of doing this, but I believe this is the most simple.

The line should preferably be a little slack or wavy when landing on the water. This slack will compensate for conflicting currents on the surface and help prevent the line from dragging. Too much slack results in the loss of line control when striking fish or picking up the line for a back cast. It is the back cast that is the mark of an expert angler. There is a difference of course, between putting out a fly that will make trout rise—and hooking the trout that do come up. Your strike, which sets the hook, must be quick—practically simultaneous with the flash of the fish. A trout realizes the deception of an artificial fly just as soon as he closes his mouth and will eject the lure instantly. If the hook is not set in this brief moment, the fish will be missed. The chance of getting that trout back for a second try is remote. When I first started to learn fly fishing, I remember spending several days on Paradise Creek in Pennsylvania, working the water around Henryville. Without exaggeration, I probably had at least one hundred trout take the fly, and my total catch for the period was one very small brownie who somehow got the hook in his cheek. Casting I had learned well, but in the matter of hooking fish I was completely innocent. This is common to all novice anglers, especially to those who learn without instruction.

Large fish generally take a fly more slowly and deliberately than the smaller ones, and this is particularly true in slow water. A big trout is likely to take the fly with almost no surface disturbance; just a tiny bubble might mark his rise to a floating fly. If you were to strike this fish as fast as a small one, you would probably pull the fly away before it was actually accepted. The speed and power in your strike is gauged to some extent, then, on the size of the fish, but the strike also depends on the length of line out, and whether it is submerged or on the surface. The wet fly man shifting to a dry fly is inclined to strike too hard and too fast. It takes very little force to set a hook, but most of the force is used in overcoming the inertia of a long sunken line when fishing a wet fly, and this resistance is greatly lessened with a floating line and the dry fly. Proper timing of the strike cannot be learned quickly. We all miss trout even after years of experience.

Short casts are usually best if you can use them without alarming the trout because you have better control over your fly, can prevent drag more easily if you are dry fly fishing, and if you are using wet flies you have a better chance to hook the fish. This is one of the strongest arguments for fishing upstream whenever possible. The trout are less likely to see you when you approach from below. When fishing from the shore, long casts are often necessary to reach the fish, but the wading angler or boat fisherman can usually govern the length of his casts largely by the distance at which the fish can see him. In fast, broken water, when it is discolored, or at dusk, very short casts are often effective. On a bright, clear day, with placid water unbroken by a breeze, it is usually necessary to work with a long line.

The *line hand* plays an important role in fly casting, and its importance increases with the distance you have to cast. In really long casts, the left hand will be as busy as the rod hand—pulling more speed into the flight of the line. But even as a fundamental practice, line hand control is half the battle in making a talented fly caster. The fact that the left hand should always be equidistant from the right hand throughout the cast seldom makes an impression on beginning anglers, for the simple reason that they are more concerned with waving the rod back and forth. This is understandable, but if you concentrate only on the rod these basic motions will be neglected.

For short casts, the left hand could be ignored. In fact, the lack of movement on the part of the line hand might even look good on an experienced caster. But our friend would never get out of the 50-foot class without a good tail wind. For the sake of illustration, we find the angler with his line extended on the water, preparatory to making a back cast. We'll say his hands are ten inches apart. Now, as the back cast starts, we see that his line hand is still in the same position, while his rod hand has moved another ten inches backward. This drops a belly of slack between the guide and his line hand. In effect, the caster is sliding the rod ten inches up the line. His hands are now twenty inches apart. This is almost a complete loss of power and speed, and, worst of all, the line is jerked to a halt by the butt guide. The two most common results are a grounded back cast or a completely underpowered forward cast. It takes but a few minutes' thought and a few hours' practice to make a high back cast. To get the most out of his rod, the angler must move his line hand *across* and *up*, following the path of his right hand.

On the forward cast the problem is reversed. Here the average caster brings his rod forward—this time sliding the rod down the line—throwing in slack where he should have tension. To avoid this, simply follow the same hand relationship going forward. Keep your hands at *equal distances* in both the back and forward casts. This is a continuous motion which puts the line in the same plane as the rod's pull. It can be likened to gripping and swinging a two-handed axe; it is practically the same motion. There is no loss of tension and therefore no loss of speed—the line and rod are working together. If done properly, the angler has split second control over his line and extra power available for a long "shoot." It is most important that the whole cast be executed smoothly, with a complete absence of jerks.

Casting directly into a strong wind slows down the forward motion of the line with ordinary casts, but this can be minimized by a slight change in speed and direction. The lift, back cast, and pause are made in the usual way, but the difference is in the forward cast, which is harder, with more wrist snap, and continues until the rod has almost reached horizontal. In this cast, the line travels forward in a lower plane, and the advancing line rolls out in a narrow loop. Thus, the wind resistance is considerably reduced because of the lower plane of flight and because of the smaller "front" presented by the curve of the advancing line.

Sometimes you find yourself in a position where a screen of trees or bushes prevents the backward extension of line when using the regular overhead cast. Or else your target is under a screen of trees, which defeats the forward extension of line. Either way you're in a pickle. I have fished many places where both the back cast and the forward cast required a low shoot to get at the fish. If you can't change position, and there's enough open area between the water and the branches to extend a proper length of line, you can use the side cast. The side cast is nothing more or less than an overhead cast made in a horizontal plane. Simply make your cast parallel to the water, facing the direction of your target. It can be executed to the left (across the body of a right-handed caster), or to the right. Obviously, the same cast can be made in any intermediate plane between horizontal and vertical to put your back cast at best advantage.

If the obstacles in the rear are not too tall, willows or alders, for instance, you might use the steeple cast. The steeple takes considerable practice to execute smoothly, and consists simply of a high back cast. The rod hand emphasis is on throwing the line upward rather than backward. The rod is raised vertically practically to full arm length over the head, and the movement

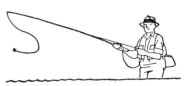

Figure 3. The side cast is executed the same as the overhead cast except that it is in a horizontal plane. This is useful for casting under trees or similar obstacles. This same cast is often used for making curves, by under- or overpowering the forward cast and putting the loop that is developed, on the water.

is quicker and more of a jerk than in the regular overhead cast. It is quite possible to clear objects fifteen or twenty feet high in this manner on short or medium casts, but the height of the back cast becomes difficult to control as the length of the forward cast is increased.

If you're lucky enough to have some back-casting room, but not quite enough to reach your target with a normal overhead cast, you might try shooting the line. Make your false casts to the outer edge of the branches, with enough slack line held in the left hand to reach the desired spot. On the final cast, made with slightly more power, the loose line is released, and it shoots through the guides, carrying the fly underneath the obstruction to the desired spot. In shooting the line the cast is made exactly as in any other, except that at the end of the final cast the rod is gently lowered to the horizontal as the line in the left hand is released. This method is used by most experienced anglers, even when there is no obstruction. It saves wrist work, since less line has to be whipped through the air, and if shot with a trifle more force than is needed, it provides a natural check at the end, allowing the fly to flutter down lightly.

If you are in a narrow stream with a tree-bordered bank in back of you, the open spaces to which you are casting are narrow, so the cast must be made standing opposite the spot at which you are aiming. In this instance, make your false casts upstream. Then in the middle of your final cast, change the direction of the rod and sweep it toward your target. The result will be that the line will describe a semi-circle in the air, and the fly will float a good distance before dragging.

Often there are places along the stream where obstacles such as brush, trees, or high banks are too close to allow room for a proper back cast. The "switch" or roll cast solves this problem. In a roll cast, the line does not travel more than a foot or two behind the angler, if that far. Bear in mind that you are not to lift the back cast into the air. First, work out about 20 feet of line by using a horizontal cast, parallel to shore if necessary; then pull more line through the guides by hand. Allow it to drop on the water in front of you. The rod should be pointed forward and nearly horizontal to begin the cast. Strip a few additional yards of line from the reel and raise the rod slowly until it is just a little past vertical, that is, point it back slightly over your shoulder. When the line has assumed this position, with the belly of the curve slightly behind the right elbow, the forward cast is made immediately by driving the rod sharply downward. The impulse given the line just beyond the rod tip causes it to travel forward before the leader and fly have entirely left the water on their backward movement, with the result that they are pulled after it in a big loop and unrolled out on the water. You can get more distance by working out slack, repeating the rod movements described here. Just remember that as more line is worked out it is necessary to put additional power in the forward stroke and to make sure that the line is moving toward you on

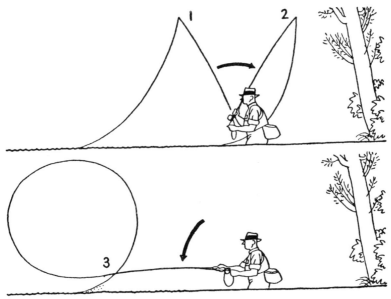

Figure 4. The roll cast is especially valuable to the wet fly fisherman working with obstacles in the rear. The line on the water must be in motion to start a roll cast (position 1 and 2); then as the rod is driven downward (position 3), a loop of line travels forward, lifting the entire length from the surface. Dry fly anglers often use this cast to lift the line in the air before making a regular overhead cast.

the water when the forward stroke is started. A good roll caster can handle 50 or 60 feet of line without too much difficulty.

In fishing a quiet stretch of water, the dry-fly angler can use the roll cast to considerable advantage in retrieving without making a disturbance on the water. However, instead of making a complete roll, snap the rod forward only part way, pick the fly out of the air with a back cast, and then make a regular forward cast. These motions blend smoothly, and when fishing a short line there's little chance of spooking nearby fish. I always use this casting technique when working small areas like pocket water or along grassy banks.

On rivers where the trees and brush are only sparsely grown, forming open tunnels among the branches, a Galaway cast is better than the roll cast, especially when dry fly fishing. The Galaway cast is one many fishermen use, although they do not know it by that name. As the back cast is made, the body turns to the right, facing the direction in which the line is going. The purpose of this move is to guide the line between, through, or over obstruction in the rear. With the line extended backward, the angler again faces the original direction, simultaneously starting his forward cast. Smooth footwork is the key factor. While the back cast is being made, as in the ordinary overhead cast, the caster starts an about face to the right, pivoting on the toe of his left foot and the heel of the right foot. Meanwhile, the rod is rotated, so that by the time the back cast is completed the thumb is underneath the rod and the reel is pointing in the direction that the back cast is to be made. The back cast in this position is really a forward cast, and the fly can be placed with considerable accuracy either over the obstacle or through holes in a wall of foliage. During the pause, the body turns back to the original position facing the direction in which the fly is to alight, and the forward cast is made in the regular way. In order not to complicate the footwork, it might be well to mention that the left foot should be in front of the right, pointing toward the fly on the water, while the right foot and the body are turned somewhat to the right in a normal casting position.

In dry fly fishing the problems presented by varying currents, which affect the drift of the fly on the water after the cast has been completed, are of especial interest. To be most effective, it is very important that the fly float naturally wherever the current chances to take it, as though disconnected from leader and line. It is obvious that if a straight cast be made across the main current to a slow or almost dead eddy beyond, the friction of this fast current on the line will immediately pull the fly downstream and toward the caster at a most unnatural speed. This artificial motion imparted to the fly by the pull of the current on the line is known as "drag"; avoiding it is a constant problem and one of the most important matters in dry fly fishing.

Curve casts enable you to get the fly to a feeding fish without slapping the line and leader into his foraging area, thereby alarming him. The curve, when properly controlled, causes the fly to drift to the fish before the line or leader, and with some practice the line will not drift over the fish at all. These casts are particularly valuable in hard-fished streams, or during periods of low water, when the slightest shadow will scare a brown trout into the next county.

The right-curve cast is used when fishing upstream from the left bank and casting the fly into eddies or slow currents beyond the main current. The left curve is used for the same purpose when the caster is fishing upstream from the right bank—in both cases assuming the angler to be right-handed. As we have already seen, in both the overhead and side casts (which are the same casts in different planes), the line unrolls in a loop or curve whether it is traveling forward or backward. It doesn't straighten completely until after the forward cast has finished. So if you were making a horizontal cast, and the line were dropped on the water while the loop is still formed, the result would be a perfect curve cast. To be precise, you don't cast a right curve. It is already formed. You simply take advantage of the unrolling loop by getting the line on the water before it is completely extended. How well you time the arrival of the line will determine how much curve you throw. There's a fine sense of delicacy in executing this cast.

When making the right curve, be careful not to put too much power in your forward cast. Keep 8 or 10 feet of slack in your line hand, and just as the advancing loop approaches extension, release the slack an instant sooner than you would normally. This premature shoot is drawn out by the line loop, which ceases to unroll, leaving the fly and leader to follow along behind. A forceful cast may have more than enough energy to pull the shooting line and still extend the loop, so pace your rod work slowly and deliberately. It will take a little practice to get the right amount of speed and the proper time for release. In very short casts there's no need to use the shooting line at all; simply under-power your regular side cast.

The amount of curve put into the cast can be controlled by the angle of your rod. The horizontal plane produces the widest curve, and the nearer your rod approaches vertical the narrower this curve becomes. Overhead casting makes the narrowest line loop, while side casting produces the widest line loop. Actually, you can't throw a good curve once the rod angle is greater than sixty degrees.

The left curve cast is opposite not only in direction but also in execution. This cast is overpowered. Again the side cast is used, except that the force of the forward cast is greater than normal. To make the fly and leader swing around out of their normal line of flight, turning to the left and downstream, obviously the line must not only extend itself, but go beyond the theoretical straight line. To accomplish this, the shoot must be checked abruptly before the moving line has pulled more than a foot or two through the guides.

When casting across a fast current in order to work your fly in a slower current, you will naturally use one of these curve casts. However, it is essential to keep your rod tip high once the float starts, and on long casts it may be necessary to "mend" the drifting line. This is accomplished by lifting and flipping the belly portion of the line in an upstream direction each time it begins to drag. Once you have mastered this maneuver, you'll be able to get long floats even in broken water.

While you are learning to fly cast, it's quite possible that a few fish will respond to these early efforts, so the matter of playing and netting should be considered beforehand. I strongly advise playing all fish from the reel. Heavy fish such as steelheads

Figure 5. This is the usual way of gripping the rod when casting or retrieving. Some casters move their thumbs slightly off-center on the hand grasp, and occasionally the index finger is used on top with the thumb curved around the grasp.

and salmon have to be handled from the reel, and any decent trout or bass should be. Usually, there is considerable slack around one's feet when a fish is hooked. Slip the line under the index finger of your rod hand and maintain the proper tension

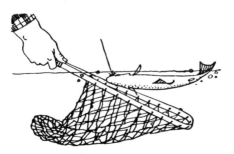

Figure 6. The best way to net a fish is to lead him into the bag head first. The net should be submerged, and the leader slacked just at the instant you are ready to lift the fish from the water.

with it while the fish makes his initial run. At the same time, reel up the slack with your other hand. As soon as the slack is taken up, let the fish take line directly from the reel and recover it with the reel as you bring the fish closer. By using this method you will avoid the possibility of a tangled line or a few feet of slack costing you a good fish. And by getting into the habit of playing all fish from the reel you will not be caught at a disadvantage when you hook a big one that has to be played off the reel, even though many smaller ones could be landed without it.

If your fish is completely played out, it will make no difference how you net him. But if he's still lively, the net should be placed under him so that when the line is slacked off a little, he will turn head-down and swim into the pocket of the net. It is always best to have the fish enter the pocket of the net headfirst, but there are occasions when a fisherman will get into trouble trying to carry this principle out too rigidly. For instance, if the fish sees the net coming in front of him, he might make an extra effort to get away. The net should come from under the water, and if his head is held high, he will not see it. Just before the net is brought up under and a little in front of him, the line should be slacked slightly so that his head will turn naturally into the meshes. Also, by slacking the line slightly the danger of tearing out the hook when the net strikes the taut leader is reduced.

If I were to rewrite this chapter today, I'd emphasize the need for a *high* back cast. True, an experienced angler can shoot from almost any plane, but I've discovered in teaching casting that if the pupil learns to make a high back cast first, then the perfect forward cast comes automatically. A high back cast is the cornerstone of effortless fly casting. It is rarely mentioned except at casting clubs, where nuances of technique are what people think about and work at. If a back cast is aimed high (rather than just flipped overhead to the rear), you have to make a perfect forward cast. The line should not travel on a plane parallel to the water. Make the back stroke skyward so it rises about 30 degrees above your head, then check the forward stroke at eye level. The clock analogy of stopping the rod between twelve o'clock and one o'clock, or just beyond vertical on the back cast, is correct for ordinary casting; however, it's almost impossible for a beginner to hit that stroke perfectly with his line under control and the rod bent.

To make a high, smooth back cast, the line must be slid off the surface. The tendency always is to lift or literally jerk a fly line upward. Because of water resistance, slack is thrown into the cast and any real control is instantly lost. The line will fall downward in the rear, and if you've created even a few little curves in the line, you'll never get a clean shoot forward. A fly line is slid off the water to a supporting cushion of air (instantaneous though it may be), and it stays there while unrolling because of the velocity which you gave it with the rod. To overcome water resistance against the line, and thereby achieve a perfect, high back cast with no loss of speed, requires only one simple movement. While the line is extended on the surface, reach forward with your left hand (assuming that you are a right-handed caster), grasp the line between thumb and forefinger just below the first guide and pull it briskly toward your body. When the line is moving across the water perfectly straight, then and only then begin to raise the rod for your back cast. Don't let go of the line with your left hand. It will slide off the surface with barely a ripple, providing sufficient speed to put a bend in the rod. Without that bend you might as well be holding a cow by the tail.

CHAPTER III

The Fly Line

IN MY EARLY days on Eastern streams, soft-action rods were considered proper for the wet fly, and we commonly fished with canes that bent right down into the hand grasp. The belief was that a soft-action rod wouldn't dry the flies out when whipping them back and forth. This was true, and under the relatively easy fishing conditions of that time, such a rod served admirably. My first few rods left me with the sensation of shaking a cow by the tail, but casts beyond 40 feet were rare, so the gentle bend and pull of a slender rod was ideal for slapping a three-fly cast on the water. It would be misleading to suggest that such a rod is adequate for trouting today, yet modern rod builders have captured great power in their tapers without destroying this original sense of delicacy. A rod can be "soft" as well as powerful, or stiff and less powerful. But one can't discuss rods properly without qualifying them in their relation to a line. Each combination of rod and line is a law unto itself, and only through a careful estimate of what our hand tells us can this relationship be understood.

A good many anglers, even experienced ones, think that the "back spring" or recoil of a fly rod adds impetus to the flight of the line. This is not true. The rod is a lever that sets the line in motion by magnifying the wrist speed of the angler. The spring theory is not correct, because a rod can only straighten after the weight of the line has been tossed off the rod tip. When the line loop starts to form, the most the tip can do is retard the flight of the line by its wiggling. The cast has gone, and obviously the line can't be pushed from behind. A short, stiff rod, then, demands perfect timing and speed. It is the rod of an experienced hand. Dick Miller tossed a fly 179 feet with a 7½-foot, 3½-ounce rod, and while the rod would be an uncomfortable one to fish with, Miller's casting at least demonstrates the potential of this short, fast lever. For the average hand, longer, not too fast rods are easier to use—an 8½-foot or 9-foot stick, not too heavy, doing most of its bending in the upper half. Long, slow rods bending down into the butt are more difficult to cast with because again they put a premium on timing. The slow, short rod is the most difficult of all. There are exceptions, of course, but generally speaking this is what you can expect.

Fly lines are designated alphabetically—the nearer the letter to the beginning of the alphabet, the larger the line. Each letter has a definite numerical value, so the first thing an angler must learn about fly lines is the A-B-C system of sizes and their meaning in thousandths of an inch. This line alphabet only goes to the letter "I" which is the smallest diameter made, and as a rule, the largest diameter the average angler will deal with is an "A," although here the alphabet grows larger, and we find an AA, AAA, and so on to 5A. For your convenience I've reprinted here the NAACC official standards on letter designations and their calibrations. You'll notice that while there is only a .003-inch difference between I and the next size larger, H, all the other sizes vary by .005 inch. Now when we combine letters, such as HDH or GBF, you can realize that the line is tapered from one size to another, and the designations give you a picture of its relative proportions. The critical factor of weight is missing because the weight varies widely depending on a line's raw material, construction, and finish.

Fitting a line to a rod requires considerable experimenting. Both the rod's resistance to bending and the weight of the line will vary. In other words, an 8½-foot, 5-ounce fly rod would give us just a general idea of how the stick is going to perform.

NAACC OFFICIAL STANDARD TABLE OF FLY LINE CALIBRATIONS WITH
LETTER DESIGNATIONS, MAXIMUM PERMISSIBLE TOLERANCES, AND
MAXIMUM PERMISSIBLE AVERAGE DEVIATIONS

Letter Size	Nominal Diameters In 1000ths of Inch
I	.022
H	.025
G	.030
F	.035
E	.040
D	.045
C	.050
B	.055
A	.060
AA	.065
AAA	.070
AAAA	.075
AAAAA	.080

NOTE

1. Sizes larger than 5A shall be specified only by diameter in thousandths of an inch.

2. The maximum permissible tolerance, plus or minus, shall be one-half of the difference between the nominal diameter and the nominal diameters of the adjacent sizes or 2½ thousandths on all letter sizes, except I and I to H which are 1½ thousandths.

3. The maximum permissible average deviation throughout the length of the line shall not exceed one thousandth of one inch, plus and/or minus.

One rod might have a stiffer action, and consequently would require a heavier line than another rod of exactly the same specifications. As a starter, any experienced fly fisherman would suggest an HDH double-taper for an 8½-foot, 5-ounce rod. If a level line is to be used, it should be one size lighter than the belly of the double-taper or size; if a three-diameter line is to be used, HCF for example, it should be one size heavier than the belly. There is no hard and fast rule, of course, especially since the advent of glass rods. I am using a 9-foot glass rod now that handles a wide range of line sizes, and it's amazing how tolerant the distribution of bending can be in this rod material. Most quality rods of glass or bamboo will handle torpedo-heads of several sizes, but as a rule, only one double-taper will perform properly.

The standard 30-yard double-tapered HDH or HCH lines are by far the most popular lines in America today. The HDH is popular for small flies on small streams, and when fishing for larger trout on broader streams the HCH will toss bigger flies. As a rule, double-tapers are used for casts up to 50 feet. If the fishing conditions demand more distance, you'll have to use a weight-forward line. But double-tapers are better than the ancient level line for fly fishing, their virtue being in the taper at each end, which reduces weight where the leader and line join. Level lines tend to slap the water—no matter how expert the angler—so the double-taper, with its lighter "point" is a great asset to presentation. However, in fly casting *it is the weight of the line* that is cast, not the fly. The weight beyond the rod tip bends the bamboo. When making the average short cast with a double-taper, most of this effective weight is still in the angler's line hand or on the reel. To lay out a fly properly then, the angler must make four or five false casts to extend some of the belly line, feeding enough weight to the rod to start its bending. On a small stream this usually results in "unrolled" casts, with the leader falling back on the line. For this reason, many anglers end up cutting the tips and front tapers off their lines to achieve some semblance of weight out front. It's far easier to cut the line in half and splice up two forward-taper lines. Several custom line makers do just that, using GBG and FAF; they sell one or the other, depending on how much weight the angler wants to fling.

The only satisfactory way of choosing a three-diameter line

is to get one that fits your fishing—not the rod. Remember, the function of lines built with all their weight forward is to make that weight immediately available to the cast. Consequently, you will find short, stiff rods throwing a GBF line just as neatly as some of the longer and heavier rods for which the GBF is usually recommended. By the same token, a long, soft rod may be entirely too sluggish to send the GBF to even a moderate distance; if the rod is overloaded, the line will touch the water in front and rear when you're making your false casts. The same effect is created with a double-taper or even a level line, in that there's a point beyond which the rod can no longer lift and speed up the weight of the line already extended. But the telling difference is that when a proper casting weight of level or double-taper is available, the weight of the line following that this casting length will have to pull is all out of proportion to the created momentum. Instead of pulling a finer, lighter shooting line such as the weight-forward taper does, the double-taper and level are forced to pull an equally heavy section of shooting line which quickly equals the weight of the pulling load.

I am not underestimating the role of the double taper, however; any double taper is better than a poorly balanced weight-forward line, and they are superior for roll-casting—a real consideration among many small stream anglers. A torpedo-head is also more expensive and requires some knowledge on the part of the angler to get a proper fit. In general, there are two types of weight-forward fly lines—one with a long front taper (from 9 to 15 feet), which is designed for dry fly fishing, and the other with a short front taper (from 4 to 6 feet), which is built to cast heavy, wind-resistant lures such as bass bugs. Even though both lines will be labeled GAF, this designation means little or nothing unless you know the length of G, the length of the front taper G to A, length of the belly A, and the length of the back taper A to F. The torpedo-head used in dry fly fishing elevates the caster from a whip-snapper to a wing shot. A mere flick of the wrist should suffice for the pick-up, then another for the false cast, pull, and away she goes across the river—straightening in the air—not unrolling on the water. Which brings us to the core of our problem—which rod and which line?

Let's take our hypothetical 8½-foot rod which we discussed earlier. As we learned, the weight of the fittings will vary somewhat, but 5 ounces or 5½ ounces usually make up enough rod to throw flies, small bugs, and tiny spinners if you must—all those lures that a one-rod angler uses. I would prefer a line of the three-diameter or torpedo type rather than a double-taper or level line. An HCG dry fly torpedo, that is, one having a front taper about 9-feet long, a belly section of 15 feet, and a back taper of 4 feet, would be approximately right. This gives us about 250 grains of the line which can be cast to 70 feet easily, and to 80 feet with a little extra effort. The distance you intend to cast determines the size and length of the belly in a torpedo-head, while the length of the front taper is responsible for pulling that weight until the shoot is completed. The back taper, like the tail of a kite, keeps the weight riding true. So actually you can use several sizes of torpedo-heads on one rod, depending on how far you have to cast. Remember, most trout are caught within a 35- to 40-foot radius, and the heavier your line the less chance you have of doing a proper job at short distances. This reminds me of the time that Marvin Hedge sold fly lines on the basis of their calculated performance. He had a line designed for 50-foot casts, 100-foot casts, 150-foot casts, and so on. Everybody wanted the 150-foot line, but not one man out of a hundred could lift it off the water. Even if you did, the line was built for extreme ranges, and you'd have to back off about 40 yards from the fish to put a fly over him.

The pick-up distance of a fly line is the amount of line you have to lift from the water for your back cast in order to make a maximum forward shot. For any given rod, then, a heavy line has a shorter pick-up than a light line. The rod and line are matched when this pick-up distance is suitable for the average cast made. A line for Eastern dry fly work should pick up at 35 feet and shoot to 50 smoothly and accurately. A line for Western steelhead fishing should pick up at about 40 feet and shoot to 70 feet. In short, the weight which you are going to cast should be extended and ready to shoot at these pick-up distances. If the belly section of your line isn't heavy enough to reach out for those long shots, it should be made heavier, either by (1) increasing the diameter, or (2) making it longer. There is a limit to how great the diameter can be, or else the line won't float easily. It can't be too long, or the pick-up distance will be so great that you won't be able to make short casts.

Although the 8½-foot rod is about the best compromise for most beginners, east or west, an angler who is going to spend all his fishing time on big waters might be better off with a 9-foot rod weighing about 6 ounces. I am assuming that it will be necessary to make casts of 60 feet or more quite frequently. Big rivers are usually the haunts of steelhead or salmon, and such fishing calls for maximum distance. A reasonably fast 9-foot rod, matched with a suitable line, will make casts from 50 to 80 feet, with a minimum of false casting. Such a rod will pick up 35 or 40 feet of line, and you can feed another 10 feet out in a few false casts, then shoot 25 or 30 feet in the forward cast. This can't be done with a light rod (except perhaps with hollow-built rods) or with a short rod. If you were casting on a stream where 25 or 30 feet was the routine distance and a cast of 50 feet the maximum, there would be no point in using a 9-foot, 6-ounce rod, but in places where casts range from 40 feet and up, this stick would be perfect.

The accompanying table is not a critical guide on how to match rods and lines. We can't take into account the variations in rod action or the differences in line weight. Some nylons now being used are as heavy as silk. I notice that the makers are specifying this on their labels—which means that you won't have to make that one size larger compensation in the chart. The new Cortland 333, for instance, is specified as a D "weight" rather than size D because in order to get greater floatability, the line had to be made with a slightly larger diameter. The 333 literally floats without dressing and in my opinion is a great step ahead in line development. At least one manufacturer, the Sunset Line Company, is now making weighted fly lines, and this presents the opposite relationship. Owing to the material and construction used by this firm, a size B weight will be found in a line with the diameter of a D. In terms of casting performance, this means that a rod now using a GBF will function properly with an HDG. I've had only a few weeks' experience with the Sunset line, but off hand it appears to be a very excellent innovation for the wet fly angler. The extra weight and finer diameter gives more distance with less effort, and it has the additional feature of creating less drag in the water. Of course this heavier line sinks more quickly than ordinary silk or nylon, and for sunken fly situations such as steelhead, salmon, or early season trouting the new line is perfect. It will float if greased, though not as well as a line designed for that purpose.

The Rain-Beau Company sent me one of their first glass lines last summer. This glass fiber line is extremely durable, the finish won't crack or peel, and it's impervious to salt water. Again, this is a heavy line and sinks readily. In Rain-Beau's torpedo tapers the light size is for rods up to 5 ounces, the medium size for rods up to 6½ ounces, and the heavy line for rods over 6½ ounces; double-tapers come in regular HEH, HDH, and HCH sizes. It is too early to evaluate the role of glass fiber as a line, but based on my own short experience, I found that it handled nicely for sunken fly situations, especially in deep streamer trolling for landlocked salmon. I imagine that salt-water casters will get the maximum benefit from a line with glass fiber's characteristics.

This is a long jump from the days when fly lines were made

of twisted linen and then waxed to make them slip through the rod guides. Later, the lines were braided instead of twisted, and enameled instead of waxed. The enamel line was a big improvement, but the finish peeled off after a while, and the angler was left fishing with a piece of string. Then vacuum-dressed waterproof silk lines were invented and casting stepped ahead. Today we have nylon and now glass fiber fly lines; we have weighted lines and even hollow ones. But regardless of which material you decide upon, the finish of that line is important to good casting. To travel easily, the line must have an exceptionally smooth finish, or the friction created in passing through the guides will slow your cast down. A soft finish is an advantage in heavy diameters (size C or larger). The hard finish tends to kink or twist in shooting through the guides. This is most important to the caster using a double taper such as an HCH, or GBG, as the heavy portion of a torpedo-head is fully extended before the shoot is made. Conversely, a hard finish in line sizes D or smaller is superior, as the line travels with less friction and doesn't snarl as easily as the soft finish.

The color of a fly line is usually of more concern to the beginner than to the experienced angler. There is no question that a light colored line is more visible to the fisherman. If it were used exclusively for dry fly or bass bug fishing and always floated on top of the water, I think it would be less visible to the fish than a dark line. However, many anglers fish part of the time with wet flies, spinners, or bait, and the line is submerged. Under these conditions, I believe that a light colored line is more visible to the fish than a dark one. In dry fly fishing a clear-water stream with a sky background, the light colored line might be preferable, as it blends more easily with the sky. If you fish "dark" waters, or waters with a heavily forested background—such as you commonly find in small mountain streams—a dark line would be preferable.

For motion picture and television work I have used bright

yellow, white, and even specially made silver lines so that when casting the camera could pick it up. I imagine that these lines did frighten a few trout when submerged, but since I use a 9-foot leader and am careful not to cast over my fish, I didn't have any difficulty catching enough for entertainment purposes. Actually I think a good fisherman can catch trout on a line of any color, since casting over the fish usually scares them, regardless of what hue the line happens to be. It seems to me, however, that the most popular colors are mahogany, pale brown, green, or gray. I think these tones please the majority of anglers whether they actually are better for fishing or not. The weight of the line undoubtedly is more important, as heavy fly lines tend to slap the water, are more apt to cause drag, and leave a broad shadow on the stream bottom. Wet fly fishing in particular is benefited by the use of a lightweight line, as it is more sensitive to the strike.

Unlike other kinds of fishing, the length of a fly line isn't very important. Level fly lines usually come in 25-yard lengths. Double-tapered lines are generally 30 yards long, and forward-taper lines may be either 30 or 40 yards. These lengths are ample for most fishing, but it is a good idea to splice on some backing whether you expect to catch big fish or not. Backing is an additional length of line which is tied in under the fly line. It should be either cuttyhunk or nylon line and has two purposes. One is to fill the reel so that it takes up line faster; the other is to furnish additional yardage so that if a big fish should take out all the fly line he can keep on going without breaking the leader. Although backing is always used for salmon and steelhead, it is seldom necessary for bass and trout, except to fill the reel.

Splicing a fly line to backing is not difficult. There are a good many ways of joining them, but the one I usually recommend is probably the simplest. Scrape the finish from the fly line and twist it and the backing together for a length of about 2 inches. A single-edge razor blade makes a good tool for removing the line finish and exposing the braid in preparing the fly line for splicing. To tease the braid loose, however, the dull surface of a knitting needle is necessary. Sharp instruments tend to nick and cut the fibers, precluding the possibility of a clean splice. Begin in the middle and wrap tightly both ways with silk thread, finishing with the same knot used in rod winding. When the first wrapping is finished, rub in some varnish, remove the surplus, and then complete a second full length wrapping. Varnish and allow to dry.

You might also splice a loop on the end of your line where it joins the leader to prevent continual shortening. Fray out the end of the line, double it back, and wrap tightly with silk thread. Use the regular rod-winding hitch. A second wrapping should be put on over the first for security's sake. Finish with a couple of coats of rod varnish. If you don't have varnish use ordinary clear nail polish.

Some confusion appears to exist as to the purpose of line dressing. The only legitimate reason that I know for dressing a fly line is to make it float. I don't believe any dressing adds to the life of the line, and, with the exception of graphite, all the dressings with which I have had any experience make a line more difficult to cast rather than easier. The cardinal rule, however, is never grease a fly line when it's thoroughly wet. Either carry a spare line and reel or take time out from fishing to do a complete job. After drying, apply the dressing by working the line through your bare hands. This helps spread it evenly and prevents excess from lumping on the line and later gumming in the guides. Never leave a greased line on the reel for a period of a week or more, as the absence of air around the inside coils causes the line to become tacky. Humidity is chiefly responsible for oil-finished lines becoming tacky. A stored line will go bad sooner than one which is kept in use. Once a line has become tacky, dressing won't help and may do some harm.

If your line isn't too bad, you can rub in powdered graphite until the line is as shiny as metal. Then don't put on any more line dressing until the graphite wears off. Your line will be smoother and better after it has been used a few times. If the finish is too badly gone, however, this treatment won't work, and then the best idea is to get a new line. Manufacturers as a rule don't like to refinish fly lines, as it is a costly, time-consuming operation. It's also good practice to check your line for rough spots at least once a season. These can be polished off with fine steel wool, but don't squeeze the wool tightly.

Fly lines show dark spots when the finish begins to crack off. Actually the line may be in fishable shape except for the places where you stepped on it or dropped a few dozen back casts against the rocks. These cracks can at least be closed. Get some Dupont-Dulux clear varnish and a large darning needle; spread the varnish in thin coats over the dark areas with the needle point. Make certain you apply very small amounts; it is better to dip the needle several times than to remove excess amounts. Allow each coat to dry one or two days. It's important to take care of your lines because they are expensive and a little preventive maintenance goes a long way.

Almost all fly lines are hollow in the sense that they are braided without a core, so the making of a floatable line depends on the finish—specifically, how deeply the finish penetrates the raw material after the line has been braided. If the finish, be it enamel, oil, or plastic, goes right through the material, it will fill the tiny cells inside and dry there, which in effect makes a solid fly line. If the finish is only absorbed to a point slightly under the surface of the raw material, the inside cells remain empty, and the line is hollow. From a manufacturer's standpoint, the problem is to get a finish that will not be completely absorbed and at the same time be flexible and durable enough to prevent chipping. If the finish breaks away, the line will absorb water, fish slime and dressing. Before long it will rot. One of the quickest ways to test the finish of a fly line is to take a few feet of the running end between your hands and give it a reasonably hard pull. Then take some ordinary ink in a cloth and wipe it over the section you pulled. It should wipe off clean. If dark fissures of ink appear, the line is literally finished. To be good, a finish must stretch at the same ratio as the braid, and if you're going to spend between twelve and twenty dollars on fish-line you should expect just that. Some of the new plastic-base finishes are so tough that you can jerk a knot into the line and it still won't peel.

Speaking of economizing, many tackle dealers and manufacturers keep second grade lines in stock. These seconds are not packaged and frequently aren't even marked as to size. They are classed as "mill ends" or seconds because of a dirty braid, rough finish, improper taper, or even for being the wrong length. Therefore, they are not sold under the maker's label at regular prices. A dealer seldom knows just why these lines were classed as second grade, and if you want to gamble a few dollars there's a good chance of finding a reasonably perfect line at very low cost. I have bought torpedo-heads for as little as three dollars which ordinarily cost five times that much, and their only flaw was that they were off-color. Of course an improperly tapered line is more of a gamble and while it might not serve the critical angler, many people get reasonable service from lines that do not meet a manufacturer's specifications. I have actually found torpedo heads among seconds that were better balanced than some of the first class lines I bought at fancy prices.

Inasmuch as fly lines are somewhat specialized, you will probably own at least four or five of them before too many seasons pass. I would suggest too, that whenever you can borrow someone else's line to try on your rod—do so. Maybe your angling partner has a line with just the right weight distribution for your rod or vice-versa. Charley Ritz and I have matched up countless outfits this way and it's far less expensive than buying extra lines. You should get at least two reels however, as the spare reel and line is a great advantage when you're putting in a long day on the stream. Usually about the time the evening rise starts your line will have absorbed considerable water from a day's casting, and with a good, bone-dry line on hand you'll be ready to do your best work.

The fly reel is usually the least expensive, and is the least important item of our tackle. In selecting a reel one only has to keep in mind what it will be used for; in trout sizes you can get one of the single actions like the Bristol Model 65RG, the Pflueger Medalist, Shakespeare Russel, or the Beaudex made by Young and Sons. If your budget is slim you can start out very nicely with a skeleton type reel such as Wards Sport King Model 88, or if money is no object you might consider the Hardy St. George. For bigger fish where you have to use heavy diameter lines and plenty of backing you'll need a large capacity single action such as the Warwick Royal, Hardy St. John, Thompson 500, or the Pflueger Medalist 1498. I own all of these reels and I know they are good. Some people prefer automatic fly reels (these are fitted with a spring and when released by a brake lever it retrieves the line automatically), and for the man who does most of his fishing from a canoe or boat, such as the bass bugger, they are a great advantage. I have a Martin Model 48, and a South Bend Model 1140; these reels weigh 7½ ounces and 9½ ounces respectively, which is little more weight than most single actions, and less than others. I do a great deal of bugging from canoes on our local ponds, and the automatic take-up helps in keeping coils of slack line out of my lap and away from canoe paddles and all the other paraphernalia that grows around a bass fisherman. Automatic fly reels are very popular on European chalk streams incidentally, where the angler is constantly using long lengths of line.

TAPER SPECIFICATIONS—WEIGHT FORWARD LINES

Sunset "Sharpshooter"

Size	Tip	Front Taper	Belly	Back Taper	Running Line
HDG	2 feet H	10 feet H-D	16 feet D	4 feet D-G	72 feet G
HCF	2 feet H	10 feet H-C	18 feet C	4 feet C-F	71 feet F
GBF	2 feet G	12 feet G-B	18 feet B	5 feet B-F	68 feet F
GAF	2 feet G	12 feet G-A	20 feet A	5 feet A-F	60 feet F

Ashaway 3-Diameter Tapers

Size	Tip	Front Taper	Belly	Back Taper	Running Line
HEG	6 feet H	4 feet H-E	15 feet E	10 feet E-G	85 feet G
HDG	6 feet H	4 feet H-D	15 feet D	10 feet D-G	85 feet G
HCF	6 feet H	4 feet H-C	15 feet C	10 feet C-F	85 feet F
GBF	6 feet G	4 feet G-B	15 feet B	10 feet B-F	85 feet F
GAF	6 feet G	4 feet G-A	15 feet A	10 feet A-F	85 feet F

Gladding Tadpole Tapers

Size	Tip	Front Taper	Belly	Back Taper	Running Line
HC10F	6 feet H	4 feet H-C	10 feet C	10 feet C-F	60 feet F
HC20F	4 feet H	4 feet H-C	20 feet C	12 feet C-F	50 feet F
GB20F	4 feet G	5 feet G-B	20 feet B	11 feet B-F	65 feet F
FA20F	4 feet F	5 feet F-A	20 feet A	11 feet A-F	65 feet F

South Bend Bug Tapers
Shakespeare Torpedo-Head

Size	Tip	Front Taper	Belly	Back Taper	Running Line
GCG	2 feet G	4 feet G-C	8 feet C	10 feet C-G	66 feet G
GBF	2 feet G	5 feet G-B	11 feet B	10 feet B-F	62 feet F
GAF	2 feet G	4 feet G-A	12 feet A	14 feet A-F	58 feet F

Cortland 333 Rocket Taper

Size	Tip	Front Taper	Belly	Back Taper	Running Line
HDF	2 feet H	12 feet H-D	18 feet D	6 feet D-F	67 feet F
HCF	2 feet H	12 feet H-C	20 feet C	6 feet C-F	65 feet F
GBF	2 feet G	12 feet G-B	24 feet B	6 feet B-F	61 feet F
GAF	2 feet G	16 feet G-A	26 feet A	6 feet A-F	55 feet F

U.S. Line Co. Quick Taper

Size	Tip	Front Taper	Belly	Back Taper	Running Line
HCG	5 feet H	3 feet H-C	20 feet C	3 feet C-G	59 feet G
GBF	5 feet G	3 feet G-B	20 feet B	3 feet B-F	59 feet F
GAF	5 feet G	3 feet G-A	20 feet A	3 feet A-F	59 feet F

Gudebrod 3-Diameter Torpedo-Head Tapers

Size	Tip	Front Taper	Belly	Back Taper	Running Line
HEG	6 feet H	4 feet H-E	15 feet E	10 feet E-G	85 feet G
HDG	6 feet H	4 feet H-D	15 feet D	10 feet D-G	85 feet G
HCF	6 feet H	4 feet H-C	15 feet C	10 feet C-F	85 feet F
GBF	6 feet G	4 feet G-B	15 feet B	10 feet B-F	85 feet F
GAF	6 feet G	4 feet G-A	15 feet A	10 feet A-F	85 feet F

Newton 3-Diameter Tapers

Size	Tip	Front Taper	Belly	Back Taper	Running Line
HDG	6 feet H	4 feet H-D	15 feet D	10 feet D-G	70 feet G
HCF	6 feet H	4 feet H-C	15 feet C	10 feet C-F	70 feet F
GBF	6 feet G	4 feet G-B	25 feet B	10 feet B-F	60 feet F
GAF	6 feet G	10 feet G-A	25 feet A	10 feet A-F	54 feet F

BAMBOO FLY RODS

ROD Length and Weight	LEVEL LINE		DOUBLE TAPER		THREE-DIAMETER	
	Nylon	*Silk*	*Nylon*	*Silk*	*Nylon*	*Silk*
7½ to 8 feet 3½ to 4½ ounces	E	F	HDH	HEH	HDG	HEG
8½ to 9 feet 4½ to 5¼ ounces	D	E	HCH	HDH	HCF	HDG
9 feet 5½ to 6½ ounces	C	D	GBG	HCH	GBF	HCF
9 to 9½ feet 6½ to 7½ ounces	B	C	FAF	GBG	GAF	GBF

GLASS FLY RODS

ROD Length and Weight	LEVEL LINE		DOUBLE TAPER		THREE-DIAMETER	
	Nylon	*Silk*	*Nylon*	*Silk*	*Nylon*	*Silk*
7½ to 8 feet 4 to 5 ounces	D	E	HCH	HDH	GBF	HCG
8½ to 9 feet 5¼ to 6 ounces	C	D	HCH	HCH	GAF	GBF
9 feet 6 to 7 ounces	B	C	GBG	GBG	GAF	GAF
9 to 9½ feet 7 to 8½ ounces	B	B	FAF	GBG	G2AF	G2AF

When I look back on the semantics of fly lines in 1952 it
was miraculous that anybody could match one to a fly rod.
As I said then, "the critical factor of weight is missing."
Today of course we have a weight in grains standard as
opposed to diameter, but I wonder just how well this
accomplished our goal? There is considerable variation
among manufacturers in diameter for a given weight to
the extent that one brand of No. 8 line fills my reel
perfectly, yet I can't even spool a second brand very far
into the belly section on that same reel with the same
amount of backing. I eschew tapers that look like well-fed
boa constrictors, but then I'm a diameter nut. However,
the advances made in fly lines during the past two decades
far exceed my personal whims. Now we have sinking-tip,
slow-sinking and high-density sinking lnes, not to mention
floating lines that really float.

I must admit that the old silk lines made in fine diameters
while retaining a proper casting weight still have a certain
fascination for me. They shoot beautifully through the
guides and with a line point at .020 inch, water resistance
is a minor factor. There are still a few old-timers who can't
conceive of a bamboo rod cutting the air with anything as
smooth as silk. But alas, the material soaks up water, wears
out rather quickly, and cannot survive the rigors of
casting in the sea.

The age of synthetics has greatly expanded the art of
fly fishing from top to bottom.

CHAPTER IV

Leaders

OF ALL ITEMS of fishing tackle, the one that gets least consideration by the average fly fisherman is the leader. Rods, reels, lines and even flies have a tangible quality or dimension that holds the student's eye and sharpens his tongue. People can and do argue for hours about fly patterns—but the subject of leaders would draw two or three vague remarks in the same company. Yet, I believe that poorly designed leaders account for fully fifty per cent of the fish that are never caught. This is a broad statement, but a careful analysis of your own experience will bear me out.

The purpose of a leader is to reduce the visible connection between line and fly. Obviously, the trout, a fish credited with keen eyesight, is going to be suspicious of his breakfast if something is leading it around by the nose. While no leader can be completely invisible to the fish, it is far less conspicuous than the end of the fly line. Being somewhat translucent, it is safe to assume that the leader absorbs and reflects the color of its background, whether you are casting under dark trees or in open sunlit water. An equally important function is that the length and hair-like diameter of a leader will cause the fly to be delivered to the surface softly—a good ten feet from the splashing line. No matter how proficient the caster, his line will splash. Even if it is checked high in the air, the weight of a falling line is sufficient to send out alarming ripples in calm, clear water. While the obvious solution is to use long leaders, therein lies the problem. First let's analyze the dynamics of a cast.

When a fly line is unrolling forward, the section which has unrolled is the only section which is pulling forward. Unless it has some weight, it can't pull fast or hard, and it will not pull the line you want to shoot for any distance unless it is pulled upon by a heavier portion turning ahead. As the loop unfolds and straightens, the front taper quits pulling entirely, the shooting line stops, and if the applied energy on the part of the angler was properly calculated, the front taper has enough momentum left to straighten its own length and deliver the final impulse that will straighten the leader.

Throughout the flight of the line various components united in a continuous propulsion of the whole—only the leader played no part. It added nothing to the cast but waited for the big moment when it was pushed forward by the momentum of the line. In actual casting, therefore, a leader is a handicap. The longer it is, the less likelihood there will be of its straightening and the more "drag" it adds to the unrolling line, which is very busy trying to get itself straightened out.

Fly casting, then, is a mechanical nightmare. Instead of throwing a weight, such as the surf-caster does, we are trying to unroll a weight. Instead of putting the weight at the very end of the leader where it belongs, we make the fly and leader as light as possible and place the burden of maintaining velocity on the belly of the line—some thirty feet behind the fly. Yet, few fishermen recognize this and continue to use leaders solely on the basis of length and weight recommended for fish of various sizes and intellect. When leaders are studied in the light of their most important component—the taper—you can realize that length and weight are only a compromise to fishing conditions, while the taper has a direct influence on your casting. Both must be considered.

The ideal method is to select a leader which responds to the final momentum of the line under a given set of casting conditions. Unfortunately, "momentum" is an abstract subject to the angler. This last motion which puts the fly over the trout cannot be computed. It comes from velocity created by line speed, which came from the tip speed, which came from your wrist speed, *ad infinitum*. Fortunately, the momentum of your cast will average the same in the next cast and every cast thereafter in routine casting, so the answer lies in finding the leader that fits you and, as an afterthought, fits the fishing. You will have to experiment with your outfit until you discover the leaders with which you can cast best under different conditions. They will vary from line to line, depending on the forward taper and the length and diameter of the line point. Once you find the proper leader, attempt to duplicate it in subsequent purchases. If you tie your own, it will be easy to get just what you want. Of course, the weight of leader to be used depends on the size and type of fly as well as the clarity of the water. When the water is discolored and one is using a large hook, such as a bucktail, you can safely use a much heavier leader than when the water is clear. Similarly, you probably would be using smaller flies in clear water, and it is impossible to fish a small fly properly on a stiff, heavy leader. So you'll have to make up a variety of leader tapers for various fishing conditions.

The size of the stream you are fishing has an important bearing on leader length. In a small stream, short casts are the rule, and the long, light leader used with the usual double-tapered line is going to cause trouble. You will have to force the leader and the fine end of the line through the air. All of the heavy line which would make your casting easy is either on the reel or in the guides of the rod where it serves no purpose. Under such conditions, a line with a comparatively short forward taper and a leader not too long will make casting much easier. A 7½-foot tapered leader, with fairly short, heavy strands in the butt, will straighten out nicely, and it will enable you to get out enough line so that you are using the weight portion, thus getting the rod action required for easy casting.

Perhaps the greatest single tactical problem in fly fishing is casting over trout in low, clear water. Assuming that you meet a long still-water stretch, replete with large fish rising steadily, none of which show interest in your offering, what do you do next? One of three things: put on a different fly, knot on a longer, lighter leader, or, at the very least, you tie in a finer strand, or tippet, to hold the fly. Maybe one of these will work. I'm inclined to rearrange the leader taper before anything else. It has been my experience that simply adding lighter tippets rarely contributes anything to the cast.

One afternoon several years ago I quit wading the main stream on the West Branch of the Ausable and went off to a shallow back-water to examine my tackle. The river had been filled with rising trout, but, aside from one fish, I must have put down dozens of good trout. Under such conditions it is impossible to analyze casting errors. All attention is on the fishing and all failure is blamed on fly pattern. So I decided to cast in fishless water and find out what was really wrong.

The first thing I discovered after a few casts was that the leader was too light for its length. It curled slightly backward every time the line went out. A strong cast dumped the fly on the water hard, making a disturbance that could be seen thirty feet away. This was the "correction" I had been making all morning. Standing waist deep in the main stream earlier in the day, my casting looked all right but after putting so many fish down, I had added a long 4X tippet. Now, casting from a higher angle, I realized this fine nylon made more splash than a four dollar rowboat because it was curling back as the fly came down. I replaced the 4X with twenty-five inches of 2X nylon. The leader still fell back at the final impulse of the line, but not quite as badly as before. This indicated that more weight was needed in the butt section so I tied in heavier nylon at that end, and my casting began to shape up. Within a half-hour my leader grew from nine to twelve feet. The tippet was heavier than before but the fly delivered perfectly; even though the trout's end of the leader was now thicker, it straightened out over the water and sat down with barely a ripple.

I went back to the river and began fishing again. Each cast fell precisely where I wished it—not two feet off, but within an inch of the trout's nose. The longer, heavier leader dropped with less disturbance because I now had complete control over its flight. Furthermore, I could cover a feeding trout almost before he had his mouth closed. When you can hit the rise instantly—not ten seconds later—the chances are excellent that the fish is yours. A trout moving close to the surface can see little more than the fly itself.

My first opportunity to prove the new leader was from a high bank, a knob of a hill that offered a screen of tall grass, putting me above the level of the stream. A deep channel barely two feet in width sliced between heavy weed beds slightly across and about sixty feet upstream from where I stood. Three good fish were pocketed in this run. The audible *slurp, slurp* of their steady rising meant that they had dropped caution for some serious eating. My cast was perfect. By checking the line high in the air, the forebelly of the taper touched the water first, cushioning the arrival of the point and then the leader. A classical stylist might prefer his cast the other way around—fly first, followed by leader, then line. This is not only a nuisance to execute, but throws the fly down hard, scaring any trout worthy of the name into hiding.

The Light Cahill dropped with barely a dimple and, as it drifted back, a heavy pale-colored fish turned and quietly mouthed the feathers. I struck hard and fast—a safe reaction when fishing a long line. Before I realized what had happened, the trout pirouetted into the roof of a dense weed bed and stood, nose down, with his tail out of water. We had arrived at an impasse on the first move. The tail flickered back and forth, then stopped. Apparently the trout was enjoying the situation.

Under the circumstances, there wasn't much to do but wade out and grab the fish by the tail. I did. But there he was, a fine brown trout who probably never would have been caught if I had continued to use the lighter leader.

The leader most beginners are familiar with is the level leader —one having a uniform diameter throughout its length. These are the cheapest to buy and certainly the easiest to make. Level leaders generally have a loop at one end to make connection with the line, but some have two loops—one to connect the line and the other to tie in a lure. The two-loop kind is a hangover from the days when snelled flies were popular. Level leaders are used for bait and spinner fishing principally, and they're a poor substitute for tapered leaders in fly fishing. I use tapered leaders altogether, except possibly in an emergency when fishing with bass bugs, but even then the level kind leaves much to be desired. There are two reasons why most of us prefer tapered leaders; they cast much better, and if you get snagged and have to break your leader you'll lose only the fly and tippet. With a level leader, there's always the danger that you might break the line point, whereas the comparatively weaker tippet of a tapered leader is certain to break if forced.

The tippet is the last section or strand in a tapered leader to which the fly is tied. The tippet section has the smallest diameter of any number of sections comprising a leader. Fly-casting leaders are designated in size by their length, butt diameter, and tippet diameter. The butt is, of course, the first strand, to which the line is connected and has, therefore, the largest diameter. The most common error in leader making is in using too light and too short a butt. The average trout taper in use today has a .014-inch butt strand, which is a holdover from the days when gut leaders were the only kind used in this country. The reason for this was that only a certain number of strands could be used in making leaders commercially, and if a gradual taper was to be maintained to the usual 3X tippet, the butt had to be light to begin with. Furthermore, there is a limit to the length of silk-worm gut strands and very little tolerance was allowed between the diameters of any two strands when knotting them together. Mechanically, the old-time leader maker was restricted by his materials. This placed a design limitation on all tapers, as they were actually a compromise to silkworm gut. Yet such tapers are commonly used today.

Natural gut in strands longer than fifteen inches is almost impossible to find, and when you do find it, it's likely to have weak spots and flats from one end to the other. Silkworm gut is rarely less than .009-inches thick, and many types of fishing demand much finer diameters. Consequently, the gut must be drawn out which is a difficult hand operation and not wholly reliable. Even when properly drawn, gut is not nearly as strong as nylon and requires constant soaking to keep it straight and sturdy. A strand of gut with a .018 diameter, which is what I use for most of my leader butts, is wiry and unmanageable. Laboratory tests also show us that in silkworm gut sizes from .001 down (these are your tippet sizes), only a .001 variation between each strand is permissible to maintain the strength of the knots; whereas nylon can be safely graduated by a difference of .002 in sizes down to .007. These seemingly insignificant details are most important. The user of nylon has more control over the material he is working with.

The basic design which I follow in making leaders is satis-factory, if not conclusive. Depending on your tackle and your style of casting, you should build from one-half to two-thirds of the total length of your leader in heavy diameters (from .018 to .014). Following the heavy material, tie in short graduating strands. The step-down strands serve the purpose of reducing the diameter rapidly, from .014 to the finer tippet sections you normally use. When using nylon you can skip .002 between each strand and still have a strong leader. The tippet section itself will be from twenty to thirty inches long, the exact length depending on prevailing wind conditions, your casting, and the size of the fly you are using. This is the only section which needs alteration at the stream side once you have the basic design that fits you.

The average angler steps into the local tackle shop and buys an assortment of leaders, and that settles that. He takes the two standard lengths, 7½ and 9 feet, in two popular sizes, 2X and 3X, accepting the belief that he has properly outfitted himself on the terminal end. Had the purchase included a variety of tippet and butt sections of various sizes—even if he bought fewer leaders—he would be saving time and money. The chances of any standard leader matching his line, rod, and casting style to give the ultimate in accuracy and delivery is about one in a hundred. It is not the fault of the people who make leaders, and considering the variables from one angler to the next and one day's fishing conditions to the next, only an approximation is possible. It is the angler who is responsible for the final balancing, and this can be accomplished only at the streamside.

I stumbled along for many years content in the belief that if the leader didn't behave my timing was off, or else the line was no good. In due course the leader relationship clarified itself and my casting began to improve. The method is a simple one, and if you're willing to take time out to check up on your gear and how it reacts to your style, it will make a 100 per cent better fly caster out of the present rod wielder.

To begin with, start your fishing day off armed with scissors and a good stock of leader material. I use a home-made nylon holder, equipped with ten spools mounted on a post with a spring clip at the base to permit the release of the desired spool. The nylon on eight of the spools ranges from .008 to .015, a difference of .001 inch between each; the other two spools are .019 and .017. This is a good working variety (from ⅖ to 3X), and the spools which hold 150 to 300 yards depending on the nylon diameter will last through several seasons.

Choosing a still water section, the first step is to start casting, gradually lengthening the line up to what you consider the maximum casting range necessary for that particular stream. This initial operation should be made with a leader approximating the length fishing conditions call for, and with a fly attached such as you would normally use. If there are any kinks in the nylon, run a blunt tool through the leader loop for support, and with a small piece of rubber massage the nylon until it lies perfectly straight. Don't start with a kinky leader. As you cast, study the flow of the line backward and forward. Does the leader suddenly flop back on the line when making a forward cast and fold up on the back cast? If so, you may need a heavier and longer butt section. Does the leader drag behind the outgoing line and gradually fall back as the cast straightens out? If so, it is probably too light for its length. There are many symptoms that can be diagnosed and corrected before you begin fishing—and this checkup is more important than choosing the right fly. Where dry fly fishing is concerned, much of what we believe to be success due to changing to a killing pattern is in reality success due to finally tying on a fly that balances with the leader, line, and style of delivery. A bushy bivisible, even though it's tied on, say, a number 14 hook, will not deliver in the same fashion as a sparsely dressed pattern such as the Cahill, even though the hook size may be the same. While the effect is not felt with a heavy leader it will make all the difference in the world with the light tippet a 14 hook requires. This is an obvious point to old-timers but it is not readily understood among beginners.

After you have become thoroughly familiar with your rod and line you will find that there are a few basic leader tapers upon which you can depend for everyday fishing. These will be tapers that match your equipment and style closely. If you don't own a micrometer, you'll have to make a note of the diameters specified on the envelope when you buy your leader material.

However, I strongly advise the purchase of a "mike" if you're a serious fly caster, as it will eliminate all possible sources of error. If you want to make your own leaders there is sufficient literature available to start you off.

Tapered leaders are most commonly found in three lengths, 7½, 9, and 12 feet. However, the angler need not assume that all lengths in-between are unsuitable. My own outfit, for instance,

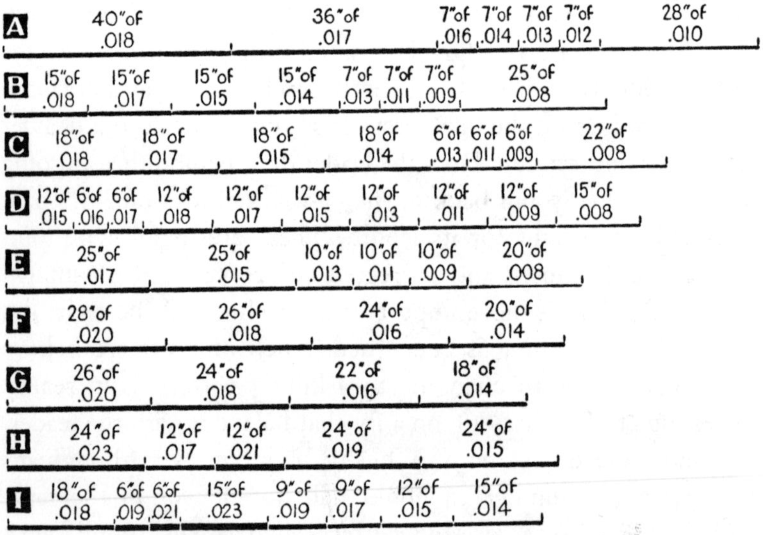

A — 40"of .018 | 36"of .017 | 7"of .016 | 7"of .014 | 7"of .013 | 7"of .012 | 28"of .010

B — 15"of .018 | 15"of .017 | 15"of .015 | 15"of .014 | 7"of .013 | 7"of .011 | 7"of .009 | 25"of .008

C — 18"of .018 | 18"of .017 | 18"of .015 | 18"of .014 | 6"of .013 | 6"of .011 | 6"of .009 | 22"of .008

D — 12"of .015 | 6"of .016 | 6"of .017 | 12"of .018 | 12"of .017 | 12"of .015 | 12"of .013 | 12"of .011 | 12"of .009 | 15"of .008

E — 25"of .017 | 25"of .015 | 10"of .013 | 10"of .011 | 10"of .009 | 20"of .008

F — 28"of .020 | 26"of .018 | 24"of .016 | 20"of .014

G — 26"of .020 | 24"of .018 | 22"of .016 | 18"of .014

H — 24"of .023 | 12"of .017 | 12"of .021 | 24"of .019 | 24"of .015

I — 18"of .018 | 6"of .019 | 6"of .021 | 15"of .023 | 9"of .019 | 9"of .017 | 12"of .015 | 15"of .014

Figure 7. These nine leader designs cover a wide range of fishing conditions, as described in the text. The diameters indicated are for nylon monofilament.

doesn't handle decently unless I use a leader from 10 to 15 feet long. A long leader suits my style of casting and carries well with the line I generally use. In Figure 7, I have illustrated nine tapers that I call "progressive" tapers for lack of a better name. Without going into a lengthy explanation over the *why* in design, tapers A, B, and C will cover most stream and weather conditions. I use A for almost all of my trout fishing. The fourth is a double-taper that can be used by anyone without alteration.

While not many people use double-tapers, this design has a definite place in casting fanwings, large bivisibles, or hairwings, all of which tend to increase drag on the unrolling line. Fanwings in particular not only drag but also twist and weaken light tippet sections. Taper E is a short, fast taper for small streams or casting into strong headwinds. For short casts and strong winds, you need a fast-turning leader, for in both cases line velocity is below normal.

The advantage of having the long, rather stiffish butt section is obvious. Considering the fact that your line point is a minimum of .025 inch (size H) and more likely .027 to .030 with the first few feet cut off, a long leader has to have considerable butt weight to keep from tying itself in knots. I have a half-dozen tapered leaders on my desk that were selected at random in a local tackle shop. They are all nine feet long, tapered to 4X; they have all been fished with and they are uniformly useless. When I stated that the average trout leader had a .014-inch butt, I was being very conservative. These range from .011 to .013, and under any condition, including a strong tail wind, nine feet of this stuff is a joke. With a light line, a soft rod, and very short, perfectly timed casts, such a taper might be adequate. But a leader has to be far more versatile for everyday fishing.

There is a distinct difference between bass leaders and trout leaders. As I pointed out earlier, the taper is the most important component, but once we step from small trout flies to large bass lures we have to work with shorter, heavier lengths. Light leaders will hold bass as well as they will trout, and the teeth of a big bass are not as bad as those of a big trout. The prime reason for using heavier leaders for bass is the heavy, bulky flies and bugs which are cast. It is impossible to cast a wind-resistant bass bug on a long 3X leader, for example. Furthermore, bass are often caught among lily pads and weeds, and a heavy leader saves tackle when one gets snagged. Bass bugging leaders are comparatively simple to make. A great many people just use seven or eight feet of 10-pound-test nylon and let it go at that. Inasmuch as delicacy is not of extreme importance in bass fishing, you could do a fair job with a level leader, but there's no denying that a tapered leader will make casting much more efficient. Bass bugs are highly wind-resistant; thus short leaders are always preferable to long ones.

I keep three bass bug tapers in stock. Taper F for use in favorable winds, taper G for normal wind conditions (from none to slight cross winds), and taper H or I for cross winds and head winds. Both of these you will notice are double-tapered. Tapers F and G are ideal for steelhead and salmon flies, so they come in for a lot of hard use. Because of the heavier lines this fishing requires, the leader butts are of heavier diameter. Most bass and salmon lines start somewhere around .030 (G), so .020 in butt diameter is none too heavy. Depending on your line, you may find it necessary to raise the diameters slightly in order to get clean casts.

The color of leaders, and whether they should sink or float, are both debatable points. I have made dozens of leaders dyed with methylene blue, potassium hydroxide, malachite green, Bismarck brown, tea, coffee, and iodine. Aside from messing up the sink, they left no other mark in fishing history. For the reason pointed out earlier, I much prefer an opaque or nearly translucent material, the kind commonly labeled "mist," for all fishing above surface or below. Whether the leader floats or not matters little—unless the method I'm using *requires* a partially or wholly submerged leader. In nymph fishing it is desirable often to have at least part of the leader floating in order to detect light striking fish; in wet fly fishing when I want the fly to work deep, the leader must be completely submerged. Ardent researchers will raise a bloodshot eye at the suggestion that a floating leader is just as effective as one fished below the surface. But this is precisely what I suggest. I am convinced that trout see the leader one way or the other, and any attempt to disguise it is wasted effort. Of greater importance is that the leader helps the fly come down looking like food. Catching trout in dead, clear water is a matter of how smoothly you pull your casts. Fly pattern and tippet size are only minor considerations.

If you really take this leader business seriously, you should have four items of tackle, three of which will be carried on the stream. The first and most important (which you'll leave home) is the micrometer. Whether it costs a dollar or ten, it matters not; you need some device for measuring diameters, and the crudest mike will at least give a proportionate answer. The next is a piece of soft rubber. This will put more fish in the bag than a dozen extra fly patterns. Before stepping astream the leader should be rubbed until it lies out perfectly straight. This can be accomplished by rubbing the leader down with the soft rubber (a small piece of old innertube will do). This will get most of the stretch out of the nylon, prevent kinking, and the resultant flexibility will cause the fly to go straight to the target. It is most important in fly fishing to have a perfectly straight leader. It takes only a few seconds to do this and it guarantees optimum casting efficiency. The third is a leader material holder of some sort. With the holder you have all sizes of material ready for instant use. The fourth item is a leader pouch or carrier of some kind to carry spares—all plainly marked as to taper and use. While this may sound like a lot of trouble, it isn't. If you sink fifty dollars into a fly-casting outfit, the few dollars spent on leader insurance is insignificant.

The subject of knots is very pertinent to this discussion. Obviously, you don't have to learn many of them, but you should have a working knowledge of at least six. A single strand of gut or nylon without knots or ties of any sort is rated in pound test; let's say 3-pound-test for purposes of illustration. The moment you tie a knot in this strand it can lose more than 50 per cent of its strength and may break under a 1½-pound pull. If your casting is bad and the leader ties itself in knots—just one simple knot—the breaking strain of that section of leader is about 55 per cent below its rated test. While some knots are easier to tie than others, the important consideration is, which knot is the strongest? The easiest knot is seldom the best knot. Considering the fact that most fly-fishing is done with tippet sections that range from 1-pound- to 4-pounds-test, it is essential that every knot be near optimum in efficiency. Unless you use knots with

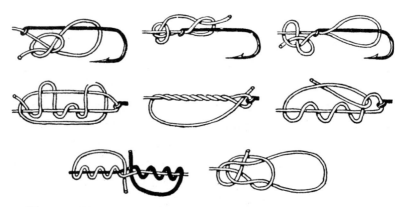

Figure 8. The eight knots illustrated here represent all the practical fly fisherman needs to learn when working with nylon monofilament. The three knots in the top row are for light wire hooks (dry flies and wet flies), while the knots in the center row are best adapted to heavy wire hooks (bucktails and streamers). The two knots in the bottom row are for joining leader strands (the blood knot at the left) and for making leader loops (the perfection loop knot at the right).

a high breaking strain, a 3-pound tippet tied with an inferior knot might be no more efficient than a 2-pound tippet joined with a proper knot. The knots suggested in Figure 8 have a traction rating between 80 and 98 per cent—a 2 to 20 per cent loss in leader strength, which is actually a safe compromise. Most other knots used for similar purposes rate much lower.

I have purposely avoided giving leader sizes in their pound-test ratings for several reasons. In the first place, there is a lack of standardization in leader sizes—the 3X of one manufacturer being larger than the 3X of another, for example. This is most apparent in natural silkworm gut, which is subjected to many hand operations in drawing and polishing. There is considerable variation in the strength of gut itself, and there is nothing that manufacturers can do about it. One lot of 3X drawn gut, for example, might test 1¼ pounds, while the next lot would test 1¾. The National Association of Angling and Casting Clubs, which has done a great deal toward standardizing lines, leaders, and hooks, doesn't attempt to establish a test for each size of gut. Instead, they set a permissible minimum for the breaking strain. While nylon may not be exactly uniform in diameter, it runs more consistent than gut does. But the diameters of nylon in 1X, 2X, and 3X are misleading when compared to gut, since nylon is .001-inch larger than drawn gut in each of the sizes from 0X to 4X; at least this is the standard set by Dupont. Both of these standards are shown in the accompanying tables. In other words, 3X nylon is .008, while 3X gut is .007, and the breaking strain of nylon has even greater range. You can buy .008-inch diameter nylon that will test 3¼ pounds, as compared to silkworm gut of the same diameter, which breaks at 1 pound and earlier types of nylon that broke at 1¾ pounds. Translated into terms of X, this is 3X--the average tippet size in use on Eastern and Western trout streams. So the X-designation is a bit uncertain, and the pound-test even more so.

Thus, the only definite figure we have to work with in leader-making is the diameter designation. Quite obviously, you will want to get the strongest nylon for a given diameter, but it is the thickness or thinness of the leader and the disposition of the various strands in that leader which make a difference in casting.

DU PONT STANDARD TABLE OF NYLON LEADER MATERIAL

	Diameter	Tolerance Plus or Minus	Pound Test
5X	.006″	.0005″	.9
4X	.007″	.0005″	1.25
3X	.008″	.0005″	1.75
2X	.009″	.0005″	2.25
1X	.010″	.0005″	3.0
0X	.011″	.0005″	3.5
9/5	.012″	.0005″	4.5
8/5	.013″	.001″	5.0
7/5	.014″	.001″	6.0
6/5	.015″	.001″	8.0
5/5	.016″	.001″	9.0
4/5	.017″	.001″	10.0
3/5	.018″	.0015″	11.5
2/5	.019″	.0015″	12.0
0/5	.021″	.0015″	15.8

NAACC OFFICIAL STANDARD TABLE OF LEADER MATERIAL CALIBRA-
TIONS WITH GAUGE DESIGNATIONS, PERMISSIBLE VARIANCES, AND
MINIMUM PERMISSIBLE BREAKING TESTS

Gauge Designation of Size	Average (Nominal) Diameter in 1000ths inch	Minimum Permissible Breaking Test
7X	.004½	¼ pound
6X	.005	⅜
5X	.005½	½
4X	.006	⅝
3X	.007	¾
2X	.008	1
1X	.009	1½
0X	.010	2
10/5	.011	2½
9/5	.012	3
8/5	.013	3½
7/5	.014	4
6/5	.015	4¾
5/5	.016	5½
4/5	.017	6¼
3/5	.018	7½
2/5	.019	8¾
1/5	.020	10

NOTE

1. From 7X to 4X the permissible variance in each gauge designation or size is ¼ thousandths plus or minus. From 4X to 1/5 the permissible variance in each gauge designation or size is ½ thousandths plus or minus.

2. Materials gauging over 20 thousandths shall be specified by diameter only, with a tolerance of ½ thousandths plus or minus.

3. No minimum permissible breaking test beyond 10 pounds.

Commercially made leaders today are vastly improved over
the kinds we had available in the 1940s. Silkworm and
Japanese gut has disappeared; and at the time I wrote this
chapter, nylon was a relatively new material in the angling
world. However, the major failure in commercial products
was poor design—very light butt sections and each strand
of a uniform length. This was because silkworm gut could
only be drawn a certain length—and no longer—but with
the advent of synthetics nobody recognized initially that
by varying lengths in making a taper, different balances
could be achieved. Oddly enough it was a British firm,
J.J.S. Walker, Bampton of Alnwick, that began marketing
"McClane tapers" in 1951 and started the ball rolling. The
great majority of leader problems resolve themselves on
one point: The butt section must have enough rigidity (a
combination of diameter and stiffness) to transmit the
energy imparted by the line, which is about one flea-power
of momentum at the final impulse.

Whether a leader sinks or floats can be a worrisome
question to the neophyte. While it is extremely important
that the leader be rubbed perfectly straight, I doubt if it
matters whether it sinks unless you are fishing a wet fly or
nymph which requires that it go under. Traditionalists will
raise a bloodshot eye at the idea that a floating leader is
just as effective as one sunk below the surface, but I am
convinced that trout see it one way or the other, and any
attempt to hide it underwater is wasted effort. Trout will

even hit the knots in a leader when they're busy gorging on midges. To convince myself, I spent time in a wet suit with scuba gear studying the subject from the trout's point of view; I only came to the concluson that a sunken leader is *more* visible with its double image reflecting against the surface when it's an inch or so under the water than a floating leader, which frankly I had more difficulty finding. Leader shadow on the bottom is of no consequence because from the trout's position, facing the current, his view of the river is horizontal and upward. To a fisherman standing in the water and looking down on the full length of it, the shadow may be alarming, but a trout has no such advantage. The important thing is that the leader makes it possible for an artificial fly to arrive on the stream like a natural insect. And to achieve that depends on how smoothly you present your casts.

CHAPTER V

Fishing the Nymph

NEVER A SEASON passes when the fly fisherman can look back and say that he made a perfect score every day astream. It's safe to assume that most days were spent changing fly patterns even when feeding fish were in evidence, and not too much thought was given to the method itself. In the year of my first fly rod, I remember fishing a small Adirondack pond, casting to one rising trout after another. At each splash I laid the fly down gently, floating the feathers through a hundred widening rings without so much as a touch from the trout. The six or eight fly patterns I owned at that time were used over and over again, and by nightfall my creel was still empty. Back at the boat landing, the liveryman showed me a great basket of fat brook trout that he had caught that same afternoon. My "splashes," which I thought were made by the feeding end of a trout, had been made by their tails as they gobbled a vast hatch of nymphs rising from the weeds. To the older fly fisherman that particular day must have been a memorable one.

Since this first experience, I've stumbled through a few thousand situations, casting to the rise of an honest trout with his head up—then covering assorted feeding activities that are not clearly defined in the lore of angling. We simplify the matter by electing a top, bottom, and middle; the top is where we float a dry fly, the bottom is for nymph fishing, and the mid-depth for nymphs or wet flies. Yet, the most difficult fish to deal with are those that feed in, rather than on, or under the surface. Few anglers are ever aware of in-surface activity. The symptoms are usually flat, clear water, with plenty of feeding trout, and a few insects in the air—but never enough of them to warrant all the fuss made by the fish, who seem busy on some invisible food. You have seen this many times I'm sure. These were the lean days when one or two trout made the fatal error, but the biggest, most active fish ignored fly after fly.

Not many anglers would find a detailed life history of the nymph interesting. It's enough to know that an artificial nymph represents the immature stage of certain aquatic insects which form the bulk of a trout's diet. Facts vary with the species, but for a period of a year or more the nymph hides under stones or

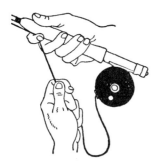

Figure 9. For quick striking fish such as we take when nymphing, it is a good idea to keep the line in your rod hand finger when retrieving, rather than stripping directly from the guides.

in the muck of a stream bottom. During this almost inert existence, trout look for nymphs by nosing among the pebbles. Often, in a sudden rise of water, stones are dislodged or the silt is disturbed, and the nymphs are thrown loose. Then it's a question of how quickly they can get back under cover before slipping into the gullet of a trout. This all happens on the river bed, so the first method of fishing a nymph is to cast a deep-sinking artificial directly upstream, adding no motion to the drifting lure.

Upstream casting is by far the most efficient way to work a nymph. The business on hand is to put the artificial in places where trout are likely to feed, against grassy banks, around boulders and logs, and in the slick pockets that show up between patches of fast water. As the current sweeps the nymph back, raise your rod tip slightly and strip in with your line hand, keeping the nymph free from drag. All you need do to make certain of setting the hook is to pull the line between your rod-hand fingers, rather than stripping line directly from the guides. When a fish takes, you can tighten on him instantly. As you wade along, watch for sheltered pieces of water behind rocks where trout lie waiting to seize their food. If the stream widens out at the tail of a pool, it must be searched more carefully, starting with the water nearest your bank and working slowly to the opposite side. It is easier of course, if you practice in a small stream. Here the indelicacies of a cast can be observed and corrected; you can learn to estimate the factors of drift and drag, to feel the stream bottom through booted feet, and more important—you can see the trout. A small stream is just as complete as a big river; it scours and turns to run in flat riffles; it washes secret parts of the bank deep under roots and mossy boulders, broadening and narrowing to the nature of its current—water and gravel all lying open to inspection. For these reasons small rivers are instructive from the very start.

While the greatest percentage of trout food is found in fast water, some nymphs and larvae are strictly slow water inhabitants, and thus we may find all the active trout in deep, still-water stretches. Here the nymphs rise almost directly from the bottom, and a fly fished in the same manner is more in keeping with the natural path of food. More often, however, the still-water fish will dig for burrowing forms of nymphs—certain types of mayflies and dragonflies, and sedentary foods such as the caddis larvae and snails, which do little or no moving about. Faced with this prospect; it takes the most skilled angler to catch fish. The nymph has to be fished painfully slowly along the bottom; as a matter of fact, fishing the lure "dead" is sometimes the only way a trout will respond.

At the beginning of the season when the water is cold and before trout have become accustomed to taking surface insects,

a nymph should be fished quite differently from the way it is
handled later on. It must be presented to the trout at the depth
where he is resting, as he will not rise to any distance to take it.
Several springs ago, I was having a particularly bad morning on
the Beaverkill. It was cold, and the water was running high and

*Figure 10-a. The mayfly nymph at the left is one of the most com-
mon eastern trout foods, the adult insect being recognized by its
sailboat appearance on the surface. The stonefly nymph at the right
is more important in western fishing. Most stonefly nymphs are
large and move clumsily through the water. They are difficult to
imitate.*

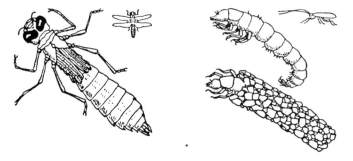

*Figure 10-b. The dragonfly nymph at the left frequents still water
and is a favorite food of large fish. Transformation into the adult
insect takes place on land, the full grown larva crawling up on a
plant stem, rocks, or a tree trunk. The caddis fly larva at the right
builds a case of pebbles, sand, or sticks and walks or swims with
its head and legs extended from the case—thus trout usually eat
both.*

off-color. Bob Harkins and I had covered most of the pools from the Acid Factory back up to Roscoe. On the way home we saw a crowd of anglers standing and shivering around the Junction Pool, so we decided to stop and renew old acquaintances. I found a vacant spot between two talkative bait fishermen and flipped a weighted nymph well upstream toward the head of the run. I'm sure we talked for at least ten minutes; my rod was under my arm, my hands warming under my jacket, and spirits at such low ebb that I had completely forgotten about fishing. As I began to reel some slack off the surface, my line tightened hard and came to life. A dark, fat fish which I mistook for a small-mouth bass broke water away out in the middle of the pool. It's difficult to say how long this brownie had the nymph, but on landing the fish I saw that it was hooked far back in the gullet.

Something about this smacks of bait fishing, rather than fly-fishing, but the incident illustrates just how dead a nymph can be fished. Most of us get too much enjoyment out of casting to use such tactics all day long, but in cold weather it's a good idea to remember that trout are not active foragers, and the slower you fish, the better. Fishing a dead nymph in water known to hold trout, or next to a trout lying near the bottom is a very old stunt, but most of us learn this accidentally. When making or buying the artificial nymph for deep fishing, it should be remembered that the nymph has to sink quickly. Some fly-tiers build up the body and thorax with fine copper wire, and for early season fishing these weighted nymphs are often most pro-ductive. In general, however, you must use a fine leader. I find that a long 3X tippet has a very slight resistance against the pull of the surface film and it slips to the bottom easily even with an unweighted nymph. This sinking is often action enough to attract a trout; if not, a slight movement of the rod tip should bring any reluctant fish out of hiding. All of which leads us to the second method of nymphing.

The second method is easier, and therefore more commonly

used. After casting up, or downstream, and letting the nymph drift for several feet, the angler works his artificial in short and delicate pulls to simulate an active nymph rising from the stream bottom to search for a boulder or weed that will let him out of the river. In the last few days or few hours of his life cycle, the nymph has to arrive somewhere where he can shed his skin, and the activity of swimming from place to place is roughly duplicated by this mid-depth technique. There is so much activity, in fact, that this is the level where wet fly fishing and nymph fishing are similar. Exactly where wet fly fishing ends and nymph fishing begins is hard to say. Both types of flies resemble various forms of insect larvae. Though the wet fly is generally winged —and the nymph is not—this point of difference doesn't have a profound influence on drawing a line of distinction. Some wet flies such as the Brown Hackle, Black Spider, Tup's Indispensable, or Coch-y-bondhu, have no wings, but they are thought of as wet flies. It seems to me therefore, that the difference would be based on whether the fly were. actually tied to imitate a nymph (thereby *making* it a nymph) or whether it were tied as a fancy or standard wet fly pattern. In any case, pulling a nymph through the water is so much like wet fly fishing that this chapter heading would fail in its purpose if we dwelled on a shoddy substitution of flies. The real art of nymph fishing is about to unfold, and if I am true enough to my craft, you might see many new possibilities in a day on the stream.

The third method differs greatly in that we are no longer prospecting with random casts but actually working over rising fish. There are occasions, especially in slow-flowing streams and in lakes, when great quantities of nymphs rise from the bottom to hatch on top of the water. Trout understand this, and certainly anticipate the event. They position themselves just a few inches below the surface where the helpless insects can be scooped up in leisurely fashion. Every fly fisherman meets this perplexing situation at least once in the course of a season; the trout hump, or bulge, the water, some of them cut the surface with their dorsals, but usually the business of nymphing is silent, with fish just sucking at their food. The trouts' eyes are focused on the surface, and it's useless to try tempting them with any fly, sunk or floating, that does not simulate a hatching nymph. Beginning anglers often interpret this surface activity as a dry fly problem, but nothing could be further from the fact.

One June day in the Saranac flat water, I located a brown trout lying off a bed of weeds. In the smooth run above, several other fish were bulging, so I sat down for a moment to study the stream. Almost at my feet, the dull brownish body of a

Figure 11. Tailing and bulging trout may be found nymphing in the same stretch of water. The bulging fish takes the nymphs at or in the surface, while the tailing fish grubs for them on the bottom.

nymph popped under the surface and with body curled downward, the nymph made two or three hard pulls, her delicate wings appearing out of the broken skin. I thought some fish would find the fidgety insect an easy target because the damp wings were useless for a moment, but the fly drifted a long distance downstream, then disappeared from sight. Only two more mayflies emerged in the half-hour I watched, and they were swallowed by a small chub who swam nervously back and forth near my brown trout.

With my landing net, I dipped up a long strand of waterweed and found a dozen greenish nymphs wriggling to get free. In size they would approximate a No. 10 hook, and my fly box was filled with nymphs that would match this one. I selected a nymph made of greenish-brown seal's fur that had been slightly weighted with fine copper wire, then wading carefully, I reached out for the nearest fish.

My first cast was badly placed. The chub snatched the nymph as it started to sink, and immediately the cautious brownie shot under the weeds. Working upstream with a freshly greased line, everything looked and felt perfect, but after covering six or seven trout without a touch, I switched over to a dry fly. The floater was no better. Trout continued to bulge and I changed patterns—finally getting back to a nymph. This one wasn't weighted, in fact it wouldn't even sink. The skimpy hackle caused it to cling to the surface film and rather than pick line off quiet fishing water, I let it drift back. Of course, a trout intercepted, drawing the leader under, and for one instant I was fast to a pinwheeling fish who changed ends and vanished.

This second nymph was dubbed in greenish-brown seal's fur just like the other, but as I held it in my palm I noticed that the fur had absorbed water, giving the body a slick translucence that filled with light. The previous copper-wound imitation seemed lifeless in comparison. Obviously my first strike was no mistake, and by late afternoon trout bulged in all the flat runs; a floating nymph scored one of my best days astream. Toward evening the winged insects became quite numerous and again I tried dry flies, but by this time there were no rising fish at all.

Artificial nymphs are built to sink—but the hatching nymph must not sink more than ¼-inch under the surface. Actually it floats in, or slightly beneath, the surface film. In casting, it must not be delivered so dry that sinking is delayed, and the leader must float except for the last few feet. Then, if all goes well, the touch of a nymphing trout will draw the leader under or you'll see the smooth bulge of a feeding fish as he takes it in a slow turn. There can be no drag or rod movement. Any motion is likely to put the trout down. The natural appearance of the nymph depends instead on how the artificial is tied. It should be almost translucent, so that the trout's view is of an insect with legs tucked in close to the body, a conspicuous bulge where its wing cases are breaking through, and pinpoints of light where air is forcing the nymphal shuck from the emerging fly. Although hatching nymphs will float for many yards in the surface film, they make repeated efforts to force their thoraxes out of water. Naturally this demands considerable body and leg movement, as the great weight of surface tension is literally peeling them out of their skins with each upward thrust. The activity in these last few minutes before hatching is impossible to duplicate with a clumsy rod tip and probably accounts for those nail-biting sessions we all have when trout simply refuse to take.

When an angler says a hatch is on, we assume that insects are flying over the water and trout are rising to them. This is the prosaic picture of a rise, but unfortunately the actual event is not always as plausible. A cloud of flies over the water is sometimes ignored, sometimes taken greedily, and oftentimes halfheartedly. We have all finished days on the stream with a sense of frustration—either seeing trout but no flies, or vice-versa. Now the "rise" of a trout is a broad term covering different types of feeding. Anglers are inclined to lump all rise types in which an honest trout is feeding on the surface. Fine points of difference have to be considered, however, if you want to be a successful nymph fisherman.

The *tailing* trout is less wary, and more easily fooled by regular nymphing methods than fish feeding in more orthodox positions. Here we have the fish almost standing on the tip of his nose, tail up, burrowing in the gravel, occupied with eating, and not apt to be frightened. Sometimes we find tailing and *bulging* fish in the same stretch of stream; the tailing trout will be nosing in the riffle, taking the nymphs and larvae at the source of supply, and the bulgers, just humping the surface with their backs, rest farther downstream getting their share from the thousands that escape to float near the surface. At such times it may be necessary to change your fishing depth, regulating the drift to suit the individual fish as you meet him.

I seldom write about angling in primitive areas where good trout fishing is easy to come by, because object lessons are on difficult streams. But Englishman's Creek on Vancouver Island runs under a paved highway, and is mentioned in every guide book as a productive stream. As a result, I have never found the water any easier than my own Delaware here in New York. The evening I remember started with two cutthroats rising in a bend just above the highway. A longish cast put the dry fly over them, but there must have been something wrong as they simply rolled short. The same thing happened with the next few patterns I tried. Above the bend I spotted a feeding fish close to the far bank. This fellow rose around my dry fly several times, taking bits of food that I couldn't see. I tried a nymph and then a wet fly, but finally my casting put him down. Another trout began feeding at the head of the run and a cast over him brought an immediate strike to the wet fly.

In the next pool above, a good cutthroat was working away in smooth rolls, taking a tiny hatch of blackish mayflies. I offered him a chance at the wet fly that had just scored, and then a dry fly that imitated his food perfectly—and finally a large spider dry fly that he bumped with a closed mouth. I don't remember how many trout I covered after that, but in a shallow run two cutthroats came to a dry fly almost instantly. My catch for the evening was three fish. On the way back to the car I couldn't begin to piece together any of the circumstances that caused rejection by fifteen or twenty trout. This was not a unique experience because trout fishermen have been second-guessing for hundreds of years.

Whether a floating nymph would have fared any better that evening I cannot say. Only one fish could actually be seen taking flies off the surface. The stomachs of those caught were crammed with nymphs, and the rising fish seemed to have something very special in mind. In recent years, whenever I've been faced with a similar problem of trout feeding out of the accepted top, bottom, and middle, a floating nymph has frequently provided the answer. Possibly it would have scored on Englishman's Creek; in any event, the incident illustrates a common situation where the angler lacks a definitive method in taking his trout.

Drag is a deterrent to the floating nymph method, but several events in shallow streams allow at least one exception. In a fast, shallow section of the Bushkill River, a pair of brown trout enjoyed the reputation of being uncatchable—with a dry fly at any rate. This is a small weed-and-pebble-bottomed stream, and the few of us who fish it never attempt anything more ambitious than the floater. The only place of concealment is behind a bush at the lower end of the run, and a cast has to be made across currents of varying speeds. No amount of manipulating can prevent drag from starting the moment the line strikes water. Late one evening, there was a hatch of small mayflies, and the fish lying on the shallow were taking both nymphs and winged flies. I caught both fish within twenty minutes' time on a tiny olive-colored nymph. Where the dry fly had always put them down instantly, the aggravated drag of a floating nymph didn't disturb them at all. This has happened repeatedly in shallow streams, and I mention it because of its exceptional nature.

I must confess that all my fishing trips accurately retold would be a formless succession of empty creels and magnificent catches—much like your own no doubt, but the allotted task of an author is to improve the skill of his reader, and having a full year to fish gives me more successes to write about. My book of empty creels would be a much bigger one, but an inspection of their causes would prove that I was an ignoramus in committing the same error again and again. I need only point at the case of the selective trout, which to me sheds more light on fly-fishing failures than any other single factor. When a big trout is "selective" the angler implies that the fish had an appetite for only one size or pattern of fly. I will not argue the point that such a condition exists at times, but the frequency of it is uncommon. Usually, there is little, if any selectivity involved—it's a case of availability. Examine the cycle of insect food and its relation to the fish; the nymphs hatch first in great number, and even though a few winged flies come over the water they are ignored for the easily caught larvae. As the hatch progresses, winged flies become more abundant. When the abundance of flies reaches a volume that exceeds that of the nymphs, the trout start surface feeding. Should the angler fishing only the dry-fly method arrive at a time when the trout are nymphing and work the water to the moment when the trout start surface foraging (at which time he will catch trout), he labels it immediately a "selective rise." This is concluded from the sequence of events that caused the angler to use a dozen dry fly patterns before something or other connected, whereas all he actually did was to wait until the fish shifted to the more available food.

Too much emphasis is placed on pattern and too little on method. Actual selectivity would mean that the trout takes one item of food in a proportion that is greater than its availability. By this I mean that if a trout had his choice of ten stonefly nymphs and one mayfly nymph, and he ate the mayfly nymph, ignored the stonefly nymphs and made the effort to find another mayfly nymph (which existed at the same ratio)—that's selectivity. In other words, his forage ratio would be ten—two selected organisms out of twenty available, or ten per cent. If, on the other hand, he ate everything, which he normally would, that shows common sense—which most trout have. Real selectivity is a factor that is not easily determined by the angler.

Late last spring, I spent an afternoon on the Meadows of the Upper Housatonic—a blustery, overcast day that brought out a hatch of cream-bodied mayflies. A Light Cahill dry was my first choice; however, most of this water is blind fishing and I saw very few rises on the ruffled surface. Naturals were soon floating everywhere but they passed little time on the river, taking off almost immediately after they appeared. One trout hit the Cahill with a determined rush, apparently anxious that it shouldn't get away. Perhaps my reasoning was cockeyed, but after considering the size of the fish I decided that fat brown trout were not apt to spend their feeding hours lunging at nimble winged insects when nymphs were obviously available.

I have experienced a good many days when large trout rushed to get the flies before the wind flipped them skyward. Fish snapped at them so eagerly that even a poorly cast dry fly caught trout. I remember one such day on the Beaverkill, when the wind started to blow right after the hatch started. Bob Harkins and I fished for two hours, getting one strike after another. But now, on the Housatonic, wind appeared to discourage the trout. Blowing off river, none of the mayflies were falling back to the water. I tied on a small brown seal's fur nymph, and began floating the pockets. For once I wasn't second-guessing. Here and there a trout would show and almost invariably take the fly. Even the bouncy water where feeding fish were out of sight produced plenty of strikes. I caught and released many trout in the next hour.

The most difficult rise to deal with is the *smutting* trout, a fish feeding on tiny midge larvae right in the surface film. The midge is a near relative of the "punkie," a trout stream horror associated with head-nets and fly dope. When you can distinguish a smut from a true surface rise, nymphing really begins to pay off. Smutting is a very common occurrence on all streams during the summer months. While the odd fish will rise to a natural or imitation mayfly on rare occasions during a smutting period, a day's catch with the dry fly will consist mostly of small trout, not the ones you really wanted to take.

There is a stretch of water on the West Branch of the Ausable in New York, along the old dirt road near Elba, that could pass for a chalk stream in any part of Europe. The legendary rivers of Izaak Walton's country differ little from this run. The flow is even and quiet over beds of watercress and other plants; the water is so transparent that low-flying insects cast shadows on the stream bed. Although the better part of the trouting here is in June, the July fishing has always been productive for me, especially with the nymph. I noticed an abundance of fish feeding that afternoon. Standing on the road where the river bends into it, I could see fifteen or twenty good-sized trout, and as many chubs and dace, all sucking their food from the surface. The rises were deliberate, almost soundless, and although a few mayflies and caddis flies were in evidence, the fish touched none of these but worked on some invisible food.

The size of a nymph is important, and more so when working on smutting trout. Midge-type nymphs are generally tied on a No. 18 or No. 20 hook, which is a bit small for the average eye, but you can do excellent work with a hook of this size, as you don't have to see the fish strike. The trout will take the nymph solidly and pull away, setting the hook. As long as you don't try to jerk the fish around, midge hooks will hold in the skin. Pattern doesn't seem to be important. The midge nymph is simply a body on a hook with no wings or tail. I personally like just a wisp of hackle, or two turns of peacock herl in place of the hackle on my patterns, but in effect you only need the worm-like body to take trout. A piece of red-brown or gray silk makes an excellent imitation. The one I used that afternoon was a tiny red silk body with a wisp of gray hackle.

The Ausable is about fifty feet wide at this point, and hardly more than three feet deep in the middle. Under these circumstances, I've always found it best to start on the fish rising nearest to me, using cross-stream casts—dropping the nymph well above his position and drifting it in the surface, riding it to him on a completely slack line. It's easy to pick out the flash of a nymphing trout, so you don't have to make too many random casts.

My first cast connected with a brown of better than a pound.

The fish's mouth was still crammed with midge larvae, which look incidentally, like tiny worms (about $\frac{1}{32}$-inch long). I had several light pulls before I connected again a few minutes later. Before the afternoon was out, I landed ten nice trout and probably lost as many more. During the course of my few hours' fishing, I met several anglers who were beating the surface to a froth with dry flies, completely unaware of the character of the rises that dimpled continuously, as far up river as we could see. There is such a thing as fishing a nymph in the surface, almost as you would fish a dry fly. It is wrong to imagine that nymphing is strictly a bottom method of fishing; there are no rules but a heavy demand for observation on your part.

A classic subject of the little known art of midge nymphing is the Traun, a pale green, serious river that wanders through the Alps in Austria. Lying over the white polished sand bottom one can see twenty or thirty big grayling feeding close to the surface, feeding so softly that they do nothing more than kiss the face of the Traun. Here, only the tiniest fly will succeed. Due to the water and the mountainous terrain, midges are the most abundant insect form, and the fish seldom show interest in larger-sized flies. The same condition prevails in a great many Western lakes in this country where midge larvae are extremely abundant—to the extent that the trout feed on little else. Frank Dufresne and I have both had exceptional fishing in the lakes of British Columbia using nothing but sparsely dressed No. 18's. However, anglers working the Traun have to buy special flies, as the smallest hook in the world (made in commercial quantities) is a No. 22, and even this is too big. Some of the hooks used by Austrian anglers are hardly thicker than a hair, but in the tender mouth of a grayling fine wire will hold.

There are a number of midge patterns for American fishing. Those made by Harry Darbee of Livingston Manor, and Walt Dette of Roscoe, New York, are especially good. Stan Cooper of Plymouth, Pennsylvania, ties at least three patterns which

I've used with great success on Monroe and Pike County trout streams. Two years ago, I began using an all-black midge made up by Don Harger of Salem, Oregon. Don's version is different from most. I found his letter concerning this dressing in my notebook, and I think the story is worth recording:

We were on the Crooked River and the weather was hot. Not much doing with the rainbow until evening when the sun had dipped behind the canyon rim. Not far above camp was a stretch of water that I had fished a few times previously with varying results. We could see rainbow up to two pounds breaking the water, in those wonderful head and tail rises that mean feeding fish. We tried everything on them the first evening from size 20 to size 8 dry flies without even a looker. After two hours of steady fishing we were talking to ourselves. In the darkness we returned to camp to await the next evening.

Again the fish were swirling and boiling and breaking water. Again we beat our brains out with no results. Just before dark Atherton cursed mightily, claiming that even Ed Hewitt couldn't catch a fish out of that mess. He quit and returned to camp. I stuck it out. After having gone through the run of flies for the umpteenth time, I discovered the little black "no-names" that I had tied for a try on the Santiam River the year before but had never used.

I greased the line good and also the leader with the exception of the 4X tippet. On the tippet I smeared a little saliva as well as on the fly. On the first cast I dropped it about 6 feet above a rising fish and watched it sink just barely below the surface. There was a good swirl and the leader straightened out. I was of course a bit heavy-handed after all of the dry runs and left the fly in a good fish. I had one left. It disappeared the same way. Hurrying back to camp I told Jack what had happened and we spent the entire next day tying up the little varmints. That evening we hit the stretch again.

For the first time in my fishing career and in Atherton's (according to him) we found one fly and only one that would take the fish. It was like fishing in a hatchery. We tried other tiny wets with no success, but when we'd put the little black thing on, we'd have a fish. I have carried it with me ever since and had it save the day in 1948 while fishing for brown trout on the Crescent creek, one of the tributaries of the upper Deschutes. Three or four times in 1949 when the going was rough it again came to the rescue. Am convinced now that when the fish are "bulging" and choosy as all get-out, that the little bug will really work wonders.

Anyhow I am anxious for you to try it back there and let me know what luck it brings you. It is deliberately dressed with the lower ⅓ of the hook shank left bare so that it will hang in the water much like an umbrella. It will never sink very far but it must not float. Seems to work best with the line and leader greased, all but about a foot of the tippet and fly.

Generally, midges are best tied on No. 20 hooks, and the leader tippet should be 4X or smaller. A coarse leader will simply destroy the illusion and put the fish down. Quite frequently, trout will strike the knots in a leader when they are feeding on midges. Most trout fishermen experience this at one time or another, and that should be a positive tip-off in case you're ever in doubt. The best method I have found for fishing the midge-nymph in a stream is to cast up and across stream and let it drift naturally. In still-water or a lake, I cast and let it sink and then draw the nymph back toward the surface very slowly. This action is repeated until the cast is fished out.

Many people tie, or buy, large-sized lures to imitate various stonefly and dragonfly nymphs—by large, I mean size 8 hooks and bigger. While it is true that some naturals are large, the chances of your getting a killing imitation are one in a hundred. I make it a rule to give the trout as little as possible to find fault with—just present something that could be mistaken for food. Small nymph flies drift more naturally than the big ones, and if you study stream life closely you'll find the greatest percentage of naturals are best imitated by dressings on a No. 12 hook. From personal experience, I'd elect nymphs tied on size 12 and 14 hooks as being the most useful on both Eastern and Western rivers, provided they're supplemented with a few midge-type nymphs on size 18 and 20 hooks.

Although Western anglers in general are inclined to shun small flies of any sort, many of the best fishermen work with extra small sizes. The fastest trout fishing I ever had on the lower Madison River was with a No. 16 nymph. This was due to ignorance rather than experience, but the incident made me aware of the fact that trout habits are much the same everywhere. Don Olson, a local fly-tier, worked out a March Brown pattern for the Firehole region a few years back which I've since had occasion to try in many large Western streams with good success. Don ties it to imitate the emerging subimago, the stage in which the natural mayfly begins to break from the nymphal case. Don's March Brown gave me at least two good days with summer steelhead in British Columbia streams—and this was tied on a No. 14 medium shank hook. This is probably the smallest size practicable for big sea-run rainbows.

It isn't the least bit necessary to be able to identify the naturals; just find out what's crawling around or drifting with the current and match it for color and size as best you can. The most useful colors in my experience have been shades of brown and dark olive. I have a number of nymphs tied in combinations of yellow and gray, and orange and gray, but thus far they have been more attractive to me than to the trout. The natural is flattish in appearance and lighter in color on the bottom than on the top; consequently, a nymph tied with a dark brown back and a yellow underside, slightly flattened, is a good general pattern.

Modern exponents of the exact imitation school, such as Mike Roche and Dan Bailey, build nymphs so lifelike that they can't be distinguished from the real thing. While such artful copies work quite well in high water during the spring months, they are much less effective in low, clear water. In making a perfect imitation, the fly-tier has to resort to varnishes and materials that give the nymph considerable weight and stiffness—thus eliminating the possibilities of lifelike action. The early season angler will find good use for weighted nymphs, however, particularly when there's a strong head of water flowing.

As a beginner, your best approach in the matter of pattern is in making certain that the nymphs are made of absorbent materials, soft hen hackles and furs, and never too fully tied; soft feather legs and perhaps a coarse seal's fur body or dubbing spun from the underfur of polar bear is the substance from which good nymph patterns are made. Inasmuch as I've found suggestion better than exact imitation, my nymph tying and buying problems are at a minimum. I chose the form I've found most useful—a tapering body from the tail, ending in a bulge at the head—and I keep a stock in different colors and sizes. Most important is that the nymph has an active hackle tied at the head. I think grouse hackle is the best for this purpose. Unfortunately, nymph patterns are not standardized as are dry flies; there are countless hundreds of mayfly nymph imitations alone —all bearing similar names. In some cases, the originator prefixes his patterns with his own name, such as the Skues, Hewitt, or Bergman series of nymphs. This is a legitimate practice and certainly lessens much of the confusion.

Nymph hooks demand another attention which too few anglers recognize as being important—the quality of the wire. Considering the fact that the typical strike is almost instantaneous and demands a positive reaction on your part, it seems ridiculous to go fishing with dull-pointed hooks or nymphs tied on wire that is too soft or too brittle to withstand fighting pressure. Yet, the greatest percentage of anglers don't even bother to carry a hook sharpener. I can safely say that my catches have increased a good ten per cent since I started to use an Arkansas stone to keep hook points needle sharp. It is surprising how quickly even a good hook will dull. After catching a trout it takes but a few seconds to run the stone along the point (parallel to it), thereby assuring a proper "bite" for the next fish. Behr-Manning of Troy, New York, makes a good sharpener, incidentally—it's called the Crystolon Fish Hook Stone.

One point I didn't make in this chapter is that nymph
fishing requires long, fine leaders. Lengths of 12 to 15 feet
tapered to diameters of 3X or smaller will raise far more
fish than the shorter and heavier ones in common use. A
knotless leader is best, or at least it should have a minimum
of knots to avoid picking up algae and weeds. To get a
lifelike drift I prefer a long tippet (28 inches or more) of
soft monofilament; this requires just one knot when joined
to a standard knotless tapered leader. Sometimes I fish two
dropper nymphs, but these on stiff monofilament to prevent
tangling. The nymph patterns themselves should be as
simple as possible with soft, fur-dubbed bodies in gray, tan,
olive, brown, black, and cream. Four sizes will serve nearly
all situations: No. 6, No. 10, No. 14, and No. 20. Except
for the No. 20's, which are dressed midge-style, these sizes
should include weighted nymphs as well as the unweighted
kind, which can be kept in separate boxes to avoid confusion
on the stream.

My good friend Ernie Schweibert recently wrote a
volume, *Nymphs* (1974), which I highly recommend for
the American angler as he literally left no rock unturned
in covering his subject.

CHAPTER VI

Fly Fishing For Bass

THE COW looked at her face in the river. Fat, purple-bodied flies hung in clusters on her neck and ears; they crawled over her bleached nostrils and walked bandy-legged in the saliva on her chin. It was hot. The water stank of decaying vegetation. A long, brittle arm of watercress, speckled with small brown creatures, waved rhythmically in the easy current, first left, then right. The cow snorted and stepped into the water just as I dropped the fly in her shadow.

A thick, bronze-colored fish struck and leaped, almost brushing the cow's nose. The startled Guernsey blinked in bovine admiration while the smallmouth did his war dance. I'm not sure which of the three participants was more surprised, for the locale was Austria, and I was fishing for *Forellen-Barsch,* which literally translated, means "trout bass."

That night I told the local innkeeper about his wonderful bass fishing. I also told him about the home of the bass—the Current, Gasconade, the Eleven Point and the White, the big flat waters of the Ozarks. The Tyrolean beer carried me farther north to a wide bend of the St. Croix and deeds of derring-do with a 7-pound smallmouth, to the Totogatic, and into Ontario on the Berry and the Manitou. As my audience increased we traveled to the land of the Iroquois, and by midnight the Finger Lakes, Maine, and New Brunswick tilted from the barrel. At some distant hour I was casting a Parma Belle over the shoals of Spider Lake in British Columbia, the obscure line of depth no less certain than that of the dark bock. My patient friends were sound asleep.

You might think that Austria is a strange place to fish for black bass. It is to an American, but the bass is very much an international character. You can catch them all over the world. Not only is the bass well-traveled, but so are bass flies. Fifty years ago all the fly fishermen needed to cope with the black bass was four or five patterns—the Colonel Fuller, Lord Baltimore, Yellow Sally, Scarlet Ibis, and perhaps the Parmacheene Belle or Black Gnat. The first four are used widely today, dressed on hook sizes up to 4/o, and when thrown into unsophisticated waters they really ring the bell. Most of us, however, are forced to spend our fishing hours with a modern breed of discriminating bass who are not unlike the wary brown trout at times. Fly-fishing for bass has grown into a diversified art.

Any fly can be called a bass fly. A bass will take a tarpon streamer just as surely as he will a salmon fly. He will suck in a small nymph with the same confident approach. A trout fly, sunken or floating, a whiskery bucktail, or a bright steelhead pattern—these are all fair game. But all flies are not good bass flies—and this is most interesting. There are, for instance, very definite color trends in bass flies from one region to the next. I have often found a preference for red- or orange-winged marabous or bucktails in streams where the crawfish was a common bass food.

In other cases, notably the Shenandoah River, black is almost 100 per cent in general favor. The reason given here is the madtom, a forage species native to that river, of which smallmouths are extremely fond. Frankly, I have never seen a black madtom. I sometimes wonder if the intent isn't to imitate the polliwog or frog larva, of which anglers find large quantities in Shenandoah bass. The madtom, or "stonecat," as it is sometimes called, is found under slabs of rock in fast water and limits its habitat to this situation in large rivers. Whatever the intent, black is definitely the color for this region. Again we find black as the best color in the Ozark region, notably on the Current, White, and Spring Rivers.

In looking at bass wet flies we find them divided into two principal groups, imitative patterns and attractors. A good example of the imitation type is the Woolly Worm which made its reputation as an Ozark bass fly back in the 1920's. Actually this pattern was first described by Izaak Walton back in 1653 and has three centuries of recommendation to its credit. The Woolly Worm is said to imitate a caterpillar, commonly called "woolly worm" or "woolly bear" in our central and northern bass states. Don Martinez pointed out that it could just as easily simulate a mayfly nymph in that the external gills of the nymph are in constant undulating motion, an action achieved by the movement of the hackle fibers in this pattern. Be that as it may, the Woolly Worm is nothing more than a palmer-tied hackle fly, differing from the usual in that the body is long and cylindrical, having the same thickness throughout its length. The tinsel ribbing is an important part of the dressing and should follow the hackle stem all the way down the hook to reinforce the feather. This is to prevent the fish from tearing the hackle loose. The hackle fibers should point forward, incidentally, so that they sweep back and forth when the fly is in motion. When drawn through or drifted in moving water, this pumping of the hackles, coupled with its somber buglike appearance, is dynamite for big bass.

When it was first introduced in the Ozark rivers, the Woolly Worm had a yellow body. The dressing changed to black after this pattern went west; but, speaking from personal experience and the experience of many others, I've found the black to be superior for bass or trout, so that the change is a good one. I'm not sure how the Woolly Worm became known as a Western trout pattern. A fellow by the name of Walter Bales from Kansas City, Missouri, snaffled a prize-winning rainbow on it back in 1935 and passed the pattern on to Don Martinez in West Yellowstone, Montana. At any rate, Don nursed it along, and the Worm became synonymous with Western trouting.

The bass' habit of picking up their food and swimming off with it for a short distance before eating is a trait well known to bait anglers. This characteristic made little impression on fishermen until fly-tiers got around to making fur-bodied patterns. Several years ago, Arthur Higgs made a big splash with his Gray Nymph, a soft-bodied fly that has started a fur-body movement. Abe Cross, well-known tier of the West Virginia area, had already worked out a soft body with a pattern called the Asp. Like the Gray Nymph, this fishes best on a completely slack line, and it is noticeable that even after the bass picks it up there is no tendency to eject the lure until the fish has moved off several feet. Both Higgs and Cross designed their flies to give a bass something to chew on until such time as the angler is ready to strike him.

To the other extreme we have flies such as the Hot Orange Marabou, which bass strike suddenly and viciously. This is typical of the modern bass attractor flies, particularly in the Southern and Southwestern States. It's an offspring of Polly Rosborough's original Silver Garland and, like the original, has a tantalizing rough, silver body. In common with this are the Dazzlers which are among my favorites for bass anywhere, any time. The history of the Black and Scarlet Dazzlers goes back to about 1910 to the Missouri bass country. Like so many highly successful fly patterns, part of the pattern was inspired by decorations on a Christmas tree. In the case of the Dazzlers, the most important part of the pattern, the body, is made from Christmas spangles. This ornament is made of transparent pieces of cellophane, some blue, some red, and some silver.

Wallace Gallaher saw the light-reflecting qualities of the spangle and, being an ardent bass fisherman, did what came naturally. After taking a 3½-pound bass from under another angler's boat, and then hitting another on the opposite side of the same boat, Wallace was in the fly-tying business. He later wrote a book on bass fishing, Black Bass Lore, and the fame of the Dazzlers spread throughout the central and southern bass states.

There are occasions when an almost stationary fly is more effective than one that is being worked. This has proved to be the case in fishing for smallmouth bass when they are moving in shallow water in the fall of the year. Quite a few years ago, at Belgrade Lakes, I put in a rough session with the elusive bass, getting nothing but fresh air and calloused spots for three hours of hard casting. I worked my flies in orthodox fashion, keeping an eye peeled for rising fish.

Like many things in Maine, the generic name for a body of water is sometimes confusing—ponds turn out to be lakes, streams turn out to be thoroughfares, a brook may well turn out to be a broad expanse of water not over one inch deep, galloping through underbrush and spilling into a lake. This one did. I thought it was flood water. I won't pretend to remember the name. It flows in somewhere on the east shore, and you would never know it was there unless someone pointed it out to you. The guide had a great deal of faith in this place, so I felt duty-bound to keep on trying.

I tied on a large Scarlet Dazzler and cast a long line toward shore. The fly had barely settled an inch when the tip shot down with a jolt that rattled my spine. The rod snapped back as the bass leaped in the air, then forward and sharp down before I had sense enough to gain line. Again into the air, up and over with a snappy kick, the smallmouth began a series of broad jumps, hardly pausing to touch the surface. He might have leaped a half dozen times before boring deep to worry the fly. I held him in hand with a gentle strain, and soon he came to the surface flashing yellow and faint bronze. He jumped again, then quit. The leader had thrown a noose around his gills.

The strike as well as the capture may well have been an accident; but, using the abrupt take as a clue, I began fishing the fly dead with no motion save that of the fluttering wings as the fly sank. Although the technique didn't set a record, I did manage to hook five more fish in different holes before dark. On the following day a big hatch of flies brought the bass to the surface, and wet flies were forgotten.

The cork-bodied bass bug first came into use on the Missouri and Arkansas spreads of the St. Francis and Little Rivers. Native swampers made them up from beer bottle corks and turkey feathers. This was quite some time before the turn of the century. Now there are literally thousands of patterns on the market, a percentage of which are worthless, but you'll have no trouble in getting good, workable bugs from your local tackle dealer. Black bass are found in all forty-eight states, and most tackle people are thoroughly familiar with the effective patterns for your locality. A good assortment to start with should include the Deer Frog and Popper Frog made by Joe Messinger, a Devil Mouse designed by Tuttle, or one of Tuttle's Devil Bugs; for the winged hair bug I'd certainly include one made by Helen Shaw such as the Rost Zebray. Among the hard bodied bugs you should have at least one feather minnow such as the Peckinpaugh or Wilder-Dilg Spook made by Heddon, and several popping bugs. Ever since E. H. Peckinpaugh manufactured the first popper back in 1934, there have been hundreds of them put on the market, but you can start with his Martin Popping Minnow and add from there.

Bass can eject a bug so fast that it's hard to estimate their speed in this performance. Many anglers feel that soft-bodied, deer-hair bugs are more effective for this reason. The soft, yielding hair is so much like a mouthful of natural food that the bass is not inclined to get rid of it quickly. From experience I'm inclined to agree—but cork does float better, and if your reactions are sharp, the hard body will prove much more suitable for rough work against the shoreline. Hair bodies hang up too easily.

Veteran bug artists learn to strike by sound, or in clear water at the instant the swirl of a rising fish is detected. Delaying even half a second often means the loss of a fish. Some of your strikes might be in the air while the bug is falling. A bass that takes a lure this way hits so hard that there's no question about hooking him.

Bugs have a strong attraction for night prowling bass. The blacker the bug, the better the luck I have, although there are many anglers who stand by white and yellow. Everyone forms his opinion by results, and results breed confidence in a lure. Without confidence nothing much can be accomplished. Bugging at night is strictly blind casting unless the moon cooperates; consequently most anglers work by sound, listening for feeding fish and working in that direction. An automatic reel is most valuable at such times, in fact it's a great asset to the boat fisherman night or day. When you decide to go bug fishing at night it's a good idea to survey the territory carefully during the day. By doing this you'll prevent a lot of headaches. You'll know the feeding grounds and the obstacles to be encountered while casting or during the fighting and landing of fish.

Nobody gets to know bass better than the bug fisherman. He must stalk his quarry with feathered cork, creating just the right impression to bring a cautious fish to the surface. I suppose the peculiar fascination bass bugging has is in the strike. To see a heavy fish rise from under the lily pads or slip out from under a dense growth of weeds to smash at a floating bug is the most tense moment an angler can experience at the end of any search. Although many of the fish will rise in the open water of a lake or river, most bass bugging is done in close to shore among rocks, weed patches, and fallen timber. To me, this is the most interesting way of fishing for bass.

I have made it a rule to never cast a bass bug on the water when I can throw it on, in, under or around something. There are many ways of fishing bass bugs, and most anglers have their special methods. I'm sure we'll all agree that the slower you fish a bug the better the results. Working a small section of shoreline thoroughly, with slow, deliberate movements, will always make a better showing than covering a lot of water fast. But just as important, in lakes and streams where it can be done —and it's possible in most bass waters—the bug must not come at the fish from right out of the air. Most veteran casters are aware of this; they never neglect the chance to pop their shots against some object. They invariably hit their lure against the side of a rock or log, in preference to the water, so that the bug descends in an "accidental" manner. Lily pads are commonly used as targets, particularly when the bug is an imitation frog; the counterfeit is plopped on a pad, and after the disturbance settles, twitched off into the water. Bugging this way is tough on hooks. The barb needs frequent examination and occasional sharpening. You'll get hung up once in a while, but usually the percentage of bad casts is so small that the size and number of fish taken more than compensate for the additional effort.

Bass can be hiding or feeding any place in a lake—where tree roots are half swallowed in muck, under bank brush, back in the heavy mats of lily pads—all places where there are weeds, bushes, or boulders. The shoreline and shallow bays are especially productive to the bugger. Inasmuch as the shoreline is heavily weeded, few anglers but the bug fisherman are equipped to get maximum results. Weedless bait casting lures are not always the solution, particularly in lakes that have been heavily pounded with plug and spoon. A satisfactory number of big bass forage in shallow water, even during daylight hours, to make surface fishing worthwhile. So much emphasis has been placed on deep water and after-dark fishing in the past fifty years that the tendency is to pattern fishing habits after tradition—rather than the problem on hand.

The shoreline of most bass lakes is covered with spatterdock and pickerel weed. The pickerel weed is a common plant in

Eastern bass waters and this tall, smooth-leaved weed lends itself admirably to holding a bug until you're ready to shake it loose. The spatterdock (yellow pond lily) has broad, flat pads under which smallmouths like to snooze, and the bug can be jumped neatly from pad to water without a hitch. By checking the forward cast over the target (just as you would over the water), the line falls without tension, and the lure won't twirl or land so hard that it gets stuck. Needless to say, casting such as this demands plenty of practice before you get the accuracy to peg small targets. Weedless bugs are a great asset to this type of casting, but they aren't a necessity. After a few casts you'll get the feel of it—putting just the right amount of check in the cast to make the bug fall dead. Tree roots and logs require careful study before bugging. If they're rough-barked and without bare branches a hard "bounce" cast might be more useful. The bounce is accomplished by hitting the log or stump with some force, causing the bug to spin off into the water. Such details will be worked out with each new obstacle.

Bugging in a river differs little from bugging still-water. Although there's a current to contend with, the technique is much the same. The bug is cast to likely places—on ledges, bushes, in the bank grass, and then twitched loose and left to drift with the current. My own system is to use the natural drift on the first run, pulling the bug loose, and letting it drop to follow the path of the current. Sometimes, in the slower and deeper sections of a river it may take several minutes to fish the cast out. If this brings no response, the second cast is "worked" by twitching the rod tip after the bug hits the water, suggesting a creature trying to get back on the bank. The third cast is more violent. Now the bug is really unhappy, popping and gurgling in genuine distress. The greatest number of strikes, however, will be instantly after the lure hits the water. It all depends on the disposition and location of the bass.

A few years ago, on the West Branch of the Delaware we

found a great many large brown moths flying along the edge of
the river at late evening. I didn't see any of them actually on
the water as they seemed to be very strong fliers and not the
least bit inclined to get their feet wet. The fellow with whom
I was fishing knocked one down with his rod tip and when it hit
the water, the big wings pounded out quite a disturbance, yet
the moth made little or no headway. This is the first time I've
ever seen an insect that one could actually imitate with a popping
bug. We took about twenty bass that evening with a small
brown popper, by duplicating the struggling moth. Many of
the fish fell to "blind" casts in open water, but the biggest bass
were feeding along the bank.

The bass bug rod should weigh between 5½ and 7 ounces.
My own rod is two-piece, 9½ feet long, and weighs a little over
6½ ounces. It is a slow, powerful action with the rod bending
all the way down in the grip. The rod must be slow, because
the highly wind-resistant bass bug travels back and forth very
slowly. The rod, therefore, "waits" until the line loop is properly
executed before it takes a casting bend at the forward drive. A
long rod makes a smooth pickup and gives a good high back
cast. A stiff, fast rod is ill-suited to casting the bug, as the motion
of the rod has ceased long before the back cast has straightened
out. Unlike casting trout flies, you have to allow a longer time
before you make the forward shoot. As a beginner, it's a good
idea to try short distances first, and look in back of you instead
of in front, observing just how long the lure requires in its
backward flight. With the forward cast, start slowly, an instant
before the line straightens out, and gradually accelerate the movement of your rod as you complete the cast. If the bug has been
fished, work it back so that just a few feet of line remain on the
surface before picking up for the next cast. If you try to pick
up too much line, you'll pull the bug underwater and make a lot
of unnecessary disturbance.

One of the reasons why I'm so careful about which bass bugs

I buy is that many of them don't cast well. I've used at least a dozen different hair frog bugs for instance, and the only one that ever turned in a good performance on the water and in the air was the Messinger frog. It certainly doesn't cast as easily as a dry fly—the bulk precludes that. However, it does cast much better than its appearance would suggest, and its feel on the fly rod is much the same as a large bivisible. There seems to be a nice balance between its weight and bulk; the weight of the No. 4 hook is offset by the air resistance of the body so that the objectionable "hit" at the end of the back cast is eliminated, and conversely, the weight of the hook is just sufficient to overcome the air resistance of the body and facilitate casting.

River smallmouths have one shortcoming, from a bass's standpoint anyhow, they seldom wander from their home pools. A large fish will make his residence under a ledge, bridge, milk can, tree stump or whatever it is that appeals to him, and stay there. If you care to spend a few hours just wandering along your local bass creek you'll find smallmouths in definite locations, and it's a simple matter to map out the season's campaign based on where the fish live. In the early morning and evening, bass might work a short distance out of their pools to feed in the riffs above or below, but at least you'll be certain of an audience. It can be a long distance between good fishing pools, so a knowledge of where to go represents many more hours of productive casting.

I have fished rivers like the Red Cedar in Michigan, where the bass population was wholly migratory, appearing only on their spawning runs; in at least one lake, Cayuga in New York, the population concentrated in one small area during the fall to hibernate. But these mass movements are usually well known where they exist, and on most streams the home pool theory is a sound basis for operation. The state of Illinois did some research on this, and in R. Weldon Larimore's paper, "Home Pools and Homing Behavior of Smallmouth Black Bass in Jordan

Creek," you will find some interesting material which gives us a further insight into the habits of bass.*

The object of the first experiment was to test the ability of smallmouth bass to return to their home pool after being moved upstream. The pool in which a fish was taken was assumed to be the home pool for that fish. Just to make certain of their findings, each time a fish was retaken in its home pool, it was transferred upstream again to the pool where it had been moved. Of seven smallmouths moved .066 mile upstream, apparently two never returned to their home pool; two other bass returned once, but not a second time, and three returned every time they were moved. In all, thirteen transfers were made, and nine of them were followed by homing responses.

In the second experiment they tested the ability of smallmouth bass to return to their home pool after being transferred in the opposite direction, downstream. Seven smallmouths were taken from one pool and moved by truck downstream to another pool. The distance between pools was .81 mile and in this gap there are twenty shallow riffles and nineteen pools, sixteen of them especially suitable for bass. Two weeks later the home pool was examined and three of the seven bass were recaptured. Even though less than half were recovered, it seems quite likely that if the home pool had been checked again later that fall a higher percentage of the bass would have been found. Mr. Larimore goes into considerable detail with other experiments, and each one indicated that the home pool theory is not theory, but fact. This is probably no surprise to veteran bass anglers, but it gives validity to the ancient angling practice of first locating your fish and then designing a method to take him.

When fly-fishing for bass in very deep pools or lakes, it's often necessary to get the feathers right down on the bottom where the fish are feeding. This is not easy to do, because most bass

* Larimore, R. Weldon, "Home Pools and Homing Behavior of Smallmouth Black Bass in Jordan Creek," State of Illinois: Biological Notes No. 28.

flies aren't heavy enough to sink more than a few feet, and if they're weighted there's little chance that they will act naturally in the water. Under such conditions a tiny spinner added at the head of the fly will provide enough weight to sink the lure quickly, and at the same time the blade adds a touch of flash which bass definitely find attractive. A small Willowleaf or Idaho blade about the size of your thumbnail, in tandem with a gaudy wet fly, is always a good bet. The lure is fished down and across stream on a long drift and brought back slowly, fluttering very close to the bottom. Only wingless flies are reliable for this type of fishing.

The stiff, upright wings found on so many fly patterns cause the lure to twist and turn in the water, and the feathers often get snagged on the spinner blade. A "hackle" pattern tied with a fat body is very lifelike and easily manipulated. Trout flies are substitutes, but they are not nearly as satisfactory because of the turned down eye employed on trout hooks and the sparse dressing. Long, flowing hackles and ringed eye hooks to allow freedom of motion between fly and spinner—that's the stuff good spinner flies are made of. Simple dressings such as yellow chenille body, yellow hackle, and a bright red tail, or an orange chenille body with white hackle and red tail, are far better for bass than fancy trout patterns. There are a great many flies in tackle shops that will fill the bill, even though they cannot be identified by standard names. Most dealers list them simply as "panfish" flies, and from there on all you have to do is select an assortment of colors.

In most sections of our country, opening day of bass season comes immediately after the fish have finished spawning. This is a period of great activity, and heavy catches of bass will be common for about two weeks. It's no trick to catch hungry fish, and in this lush spell many novice bass fishermen will learn their trade. When bass bite anything and everything, naturally people get the idea that they're easy to catch. But the very next trip might be a complete dud. As the weather gets warmer and food gets more abundant the fish are going to settle back to normal, cautious feeding. This is the time for a change of pace. The test of a real angler is not how many fish he brings in on one trip, but how consistently he takes home some fish.

There are few kinds of fishing comparable to catching bass with a dry fly. In some respects, the river bass is superior to the brown trout. At times he will rise to anything that looks like an insect, and with such dash that he leaves little doubt in the mind of an angler how he should be caught. Trout are more conservative in their opinions; even the smaller ones provide no quick or easy game for the novice fly fisherman. If I were to recommend a location for the beginner to learn dry fly fundamentals, it would most certainly be on a bass stream.

Bass of shallow lakes are also willing risers. I've spent many a hot July afternoon teasing bigmouths to the top when other methods of fishing were at low ebb. The ideal water is a weed and stump ridden bass "pond," and the perfect moment is under a bright summer sun. Beyond this we can draw a line of decreasing returns. Deep water lakes are not regularly productive to the dry fly, and even in the twilight hours when bass are surfacing, a bug or popping plug will take the largest fish. But here again, many people are apt to draw the wrong conclusions from an evening session spent bugging on a bass pond—just as they develop bass lore from experiences with recently spawned fish. Regardless of his rowdy nature, the bronzeback is just as flexible in his appetites as the trout. Bass fishing has changed a lot in the past decade. Time was when bass could be caught on very crude baits. Anybody who ever carved his initials on the kitchen table qualified as a plug maker. But as bass and bass fishermen got older and wiser, the demand for small, delicately balanced lures put the penknife artist out of business. It's no secret that ¼-ounce baits are the rage right now, and that bass fishing is fast becoming a calculated game. Even bass bugs are less primitive. Wariness among fish is born of experience, and it's easy to realize that most bass get their education at the hands of a plug artist or a bass bugger, and therefore a change of pace is essential. Now dry fly fishing is not an ordinary method of taking bass. It isn't even feasible except for a comparatively short period during the season. But there are no hard and fast rules in angling, and even the least likely candidate for a floating fly—the Florida bass—has proven an avid fly smasher in off moments. I often have the feeling that a bass rising to a floater is seeing an insect imitation for the first time in his life.

One of the finest scientific papers ever done on the feeding habits of smallmouth bass is "A Quantitative Study of the Smallmouth Black Bass *Micropterus dolomieu*, In Three Eastern Streams," by Eugene W. Surber.* The purpose in compiling this information was to study the types of food eaten by river bass, and the relative importance of different food items. To quote Mr. Surber, "Seasonal studies of adult diets would no doubt reveal important differences in the feeding habits of the adult smallmouth bass in these rivers. Specimens caught in the Cacapon River in mid-July had consumed adult damsel flies to a large extent, and there is little doubt that the time of emergence of various aquatic or terrestrial insects has a great deal to do with the nature of the food of adult smallmouth bass in the Cacapon River and the South Branch. Even in the Shenandoah River large smallmouth bass rise to minute mayflies or small black ants blown into the water from the land. At such times these large smallmouth bass did not evince much interest in artificial lures offered them, and their feeding was probably more in sport than because of true hunger. In the Shenandoah River, there definitely are times when the adult smallmouth bass will not take artificial lures, particularly after several weeks of clear water conditions."

I assume that when Mr. Surber says that Shenandoah bass

* *Transactions of the American Fisheries Society*, Vol. 70, 1940.

won't take artificial lures, his reference is to the larger baits, not small insect imitations. In my own experience, and this on at least a dozen bass streams in the past twenty years, such a phenomenon is a certainty—fishing just stops dead, and invariably the dry fly will harvest a real basket of fish. There are other lures and methods that will pay off, such as the marabou streamer, the three wet fly cast, and the fly-and-spinner combination. These are time-honored procedures used by some of the most skilled bass anglers in the country today. They belong in your bag of tricks also, but never think that any one lure or method is the perfect answer. The dry fly fits into our scheme of angling because it definitely has a period of productivity—not only on the Shenandoah, but every other bass stream I've sampled. I have never taken a really large bass on the dry fly. In fact, I sometimes wonder if I ever will. The heaviest fish to come to my floaters were a 4-pound smallmouth, and a $3\frac{1}{2}$-pound largemouth. Out of the many hundreds of fly-caught bass, the record hardly supports my favorite method of fishing for them. Yet, two things are important here which weights wouldn't show. First, almost all of the fish were taken at a time when bass fishing was in a complete slump, and other methods failed completely. Secondly, even a 2-pound bass is a mean customer on a light fly rod. To cast a bass bug, for instance, we need a fairly heavy rod. An air-resistant bug demands a powerful lever to propel it to a fishable distance. This is not true of the dry fly. You can use any rod that will handle a comfortable line. I've been using an 8-foot, $4\frac{1}{2}$-ounce rod with a double-taper HDH nylon line, and leaders tapered to 2X. I would go even lighter if our wading conditions were better locally, but in hip-deep water an extra foot in rod length helps to keep the back cast high. A 2-pound smallmouth is above average in these streams; thus the chance to employ regular trout tackle is most welcome.

It is most advantageous to use a fairly large fly, as dry flies go, not smaller than a No. 10, and preferably a No. 6. It is easier to keep a sizable fly floating, and of course the larger fly is easier to see on the water, a matter which is most important to the beginner. Under most conditions, flies of the bivisible type will float easily, stand abuse, and take bass. The Brown and Black Bivisibles are excellent patterns, and can be counted on to perform in any lake or stream. Hairwing patterns such as the Gray Wulff and White Wulff, and patterns with clipped hair bodies such as the White Winged McDougal and White Winged Black Gnat are also useful. It is wise to avoid fancy patterns and those made of fragile materials—bass are not very critical, but they do have rough mouths.

The most obvious difference between dry fly for largemouth bass and one for smallmouth bass is the size. The floater for largemouths should be larger, more bushy than a smallmouth pattern. I think the best example of a proper bigmouth fly is the Powder Puff, which was made public by Fred Geist in 1944. Although few fly-tiers have the patience to wrap and push bunches of deer hair together, the fly is infinitely superior to the hairwing and in many situations far better than the orthodox bass bug. The Powder Puff is made in the same fashion that deer hair, mice, and frogs are tied; the hair is packed tightly around the hook, then pushed along the shank as each new bunch is secured. Instead of trimming the hair short to make a mouse or frog form, the bristles are left long. As a result, the fly looks like a powder puff. Whether this fits the definition of a fly or not, the Powder Puff casts like one. It has little weight or air resistance, sits down gently, and "works" on the water after a few twitches of the rod tip. Geist's brain child has a long record of bass killing and belongs in the kit of every fly rod angler.

Prima donna of the smallmouth flies, and I say this with no reservation, is the sparse Muddler Minnow. In August of 1949, I wrote an article for *Field & Stream* called "Bass Flies, Old and New." Among the new ones was a pattern known as the Muddler Minnow, a fly tied by Don Gapen in Nipigon, Ontario.

Don's intention was an imitation of the darter minnow, a streamer for big trout. It proved to be excellent for big square-tails. According to my notes, the Muddler accounted for more than twenty brook trout of over 4 pounds during the time I used it. However, I used this "streamer" as a dry fly.

Guy Kibbee and I were fishing a small Quebec pond the first time I tested the Muddler. A few large trout were breaking in close to shore, and we took turns working them over—five min-utes at the paddle and five with the rod. Neither of us seemed to have what the fish wanted, and then I remembered Don's new fly. My next cast put the slim brown Muddler beyond a rising trout, and I jerked the line to make it sink. The fly went down, then bobbed up again. I pulled the line harder, but the deer hair hackle kept popping back up. On the sixth or seventh pull a 5½-pound brook trout sucked the fly under. But this was only the beginning. We took more than ten trout that day, and none were less than 4 pounds, and one weighed over 6 pounds. I should qualify this by saying that this particular lake holds plenty of squaretails weighing over 4 pounds, but they are very tem-peramental surface feeders. In any event, Guy and I were con-vinced that Don had inadvertently created a terrific trout dry fly.

There was something about the Muddler, though, that smacked of smallmouth, and that was the reason why this pattern was introduced in an article on bass flies. We weren't disappointed. Right after I came back from Quebec, I went to work on a num-ber of heavily fished bass waters, and in the light of my fishing since that time, I would rate this pattern as a most reliable small-mouth fly. The Muddler has Impali hair wings, and placed on both sides of the hair are matched fibers of turkey quill which should be like bustard color. The hackle is made by holding a bunch of deer hair, about a quarter of an inch in diameter, on top of the hook next to the eye. Then you take several loose turns around the hair with your tying thread, which should be pulled snugly, releasing the hair from your fingers at the same time. The body consists of nothing more than a few turns of flat gold tinsel, and the overall effect is a slim, sparsely tied streamer. The tail, incidentally, is a bustard color fiber of turkey wing quill. But the ingredients and shape have excellent floating qualities.

Action usually makes the difference between drawing bass to the fly or taking nothing. This fact was brought home very forcefully some years ago when I was fishing a shallow, stumpy pond in Connecticut. My experience with pond trout taught me that the fly should be left to work for itself; a minimum of movement usually gives the best results. So I cast a fly into every nook and corner of the pond that morning, letting it rest quietly and bringing it back very slowly. A few small bass and a number of bluegills found this retrieve interesting enough, but I wasn't getting the response expected. Finally I tried jerking the big Black Bivisible along the surface, and largemouths popped up all over the place.

When coming to a hatch of mayflies, bass are no different than trout. The feeding is splashy, but certain, and a good float will take your fish. If the bass are after damsel flies or dragonflies, you'll find that casting downstream, coming back with a fast jumping retrieve, is more effective. In a pond the same simulated flight of these strong winged insects can be deadly. With no feeding fish in evidence, I use a two-fly cast, which I find one of the most dependable ways of moving bass on a slow day.

The two-fly cast is usually accomplished with a pair of bivisibles. The flies are tossed downstream, allowed to float for a few seconds, and then bounced back like a pair of crazy moths. It's a good method in summer water, not only for rivers but for lakes as well. On the particular afternoon in mind, I tied on a pair of Muddlers, a No. 6 at the point and a No. 10 on the dropper. The heavier fly on the point helps straighten the cast out. Syd Field and I were on the run above the Crazy Man

Hole. This part of the Delaware's West Branch is flat, and the long cliff-bordered pool was mirror calm. We have a fishing arrangement designed to help angling editors collect useful material, so Syd started at the lower end of the run with an identical two-fly cast. He worked his flies upstream, using a natural drift, imparting no motion to his flies. I started at the head of the run, casting downstream, and skidding the flies back. At the end of the first round seven nice smallmouths had gobbled the downstream casts, and only one came to Syd's drift. I waded back upstream using the drift, and this time Syd worked his two flies downstream. He took five bass and I caught a chub. We actually did this over and over again in various parts of the river, and the downstream man always nailed more and larger bass.

In fast water, I've found that fishing the dry fly downstream is by far the easiest and most effective way of taking bass. No attempt need be made to get a drag-free float. Simply get enough line out to cover that place that looks like a possibility and let the fly bounce back over the surface, holding your rod high and retrieving rather slowly. I prefer a light, double-tapered line for all bass dry fly work, because when the line is thoroughly greased it has practically no resistance in the current. The bug angler's three-diameter line has far too much weight up forward to do this same job smoothly. Bass are not inclined to rush at a fast-drifting fly such as we get with an upstream cast, but seemingly prefer one that is deliberately teased over the surface. This is contrary to general dry fly practice, but effective nevertheless. In flat water the upstream toss with its omission of drag is probably the better way, yet even here there seems to be some room for experiment.

Modern American bass fishing is chiefly a plastic worm, spinner, and plug game which, Lord knows, produces quantities of big fish. However, sooner or later one loses interest in number and size, and I highly commend that if you haven't done so, go after bass with the fly rod. You can find excellent fishing during early June in southeast Maine when the smallmouths take bugs and flies, or during the early fall season on Pennsylvania's upper Susquehanna River where dry patterns can be most effective. There is some wonderful fly fishing to be had on the Flint River in Georgia, the Snake River in Idaho, and the turbulent Winnipeg River in Manitoba. And virtually any southern impoundment can produce fast surface action in the spring season when bass are inshore.

I am even more convinced today than when I wrote this chapter that fishing for bass with a fly as opposed to a floating bug is far more effective than is generally realized. Weedless streamer patterns, dressed either in Ruff Neck style or on keel hooks, are deadly in snag-filled waters. Even in our densely weeded lakes at home in Florida the streamer accounts for very large bass, although comparatively few anglers use the method. The largemouths in south Florida feed heavily on freshwater shrimp (*Mysis*), particularly in the late spring when a small silver-bodied streamer with a short bucktail wing is extremely effective. The major food form of the redeye bass in the Flint River is hellgrammites, and here a large black dubbed-fur nymph is much in favor.

Taking bass on the fly rod is not a hit-and-miss proposition, but a regional study that becomes more fascinating with the years.

Of course I haven't changed my mind about the Muddler Minnow as a bass fly or any other kind of fly. It even takes bonefish. But I am amused now at Wallace Gallaher's Dazzler flies of 1910. No need to use Christmas tree decorations any more—just read Mylar. The smallmouth bass, incidentally, is no longer found in Austria. The fish was introduced rather widely in Europe during the 1880s—from England, then to France, Belgium, Germany, Austria, Poland, and even Norway. In most cases it didn't thrive due to low annual water temperatures, although the fish still occur in the Semois River of Belgium. Austria abandoned the bass in the postwar years in favor of trout and grayling management. Probably the best smallmouth fishing outside of North America is found in South Africa.

CHAPTER VII

The Dry Fly, Upstream and Down

To BE A dry fly fisherman all you will need in the beginning are four flies—a bivisible, a spider, a bunched wing pattern, and a fly with white wings that you can see at dusk. You will want more than four patterns of course, but the secret of success in floating flies is to be ready with the type of artificial that suggests an insect form and at the same time fits the water you are fishing. From the basic four you can build a box based on your experience and the experiments of others. The value of certain patterns may change from one stream to the next, or even one day to the next, but as a practical angler you will want to give your future some direction.

Charles Ritz, a man with over thirty years of experience, represents the "functional" school. He uses a series of bivisibles in pink, gray, white, black, brown, and yellow, all designed for visibility rather than imitation. The colors are selected according to the prevailing light conditions. When the sun is angular and fairly burning into his eyes, the dark, black bivisible is by far the easiest to see. In calm water with a strong back lighting, a pale colored fly is best. Intermediate shades, such as pink and yellow, fit in when strong reflections from bank foliage create a changing surface for the fly to drift over. Each color, or pattern is tied in two different styles—one sparse for slick water and rising fish, and the other tied full, to bounce on fast water as an attractor. Perhaps Charles is an unkind realist in this simplification, but he's one of the craftiest fly-fishermen who ever duped a trout.

We were fishing a broad stretch of the Neversink one evening. The flat was more crowded than usual—and nobody had been taking fish. A hatch of flies came over the water about dusk, and up at the head of the flat I saw Charley lay out a long cast and hook a heavy brown who kicked up quite a rumpus. The fellow fishing below him asked what fly he was using and Charles allowed that it was a Coachman. In a moment the word that binds all anglers sounded like drums along the Mohawk—everybody was passing the information on. There was a clicking of fly boxes and some streamside swapping, and I know for a fact that two people fishing just below me caught trout soon afterward. I fished for a while and finally walked up in time to see Charley net his third trout. While admiring his catch I noticed the fly in the trout's jaw—it was a scraggly white bivisible. He avoided my glance and watched the shapeless figures shooting their lines at the growing darkness. We didn't speak for several minutes, until one angler let out a whoop of victory; then Charley remarked quite casually, "Everybody has faith in the Coachman."

Going to the other extreme, I often fish with a fellow who has an imitation for everything that flies over a trout stream. He not only carries a gross of patterns, but a fly tying kit as well. On a warm spring day, when the mayflies are falling like snow, Ray Neidig will sit down and match the whims of nature, bug for bug. Sometimes he squeezes a fact to fit a theory, but he takes brown trout with uncanny skill. Another chap, Lee Allen, uses just one fly pattern, the Leadwing Coachman, simply because the fly doesn't look like anything in particular but everything in general. This is probably the most radical attitude a man might develop after thirty years of fishing, but Lee works on the hardest fished streams in the East—and his reputation for taking big fish is well founded.

The schools of thought that fall between the extremes of these three men are infinite, and taken at their face value it would seem that somebody has to be wrong. If you stop to analyze each, however, without getting involved in what the trout sees or thinks, vagrant facts begin to make sense. Charles, for instance, is a genuine seventy-five-foot-or-better caster, and considering the fact that he never gets near a trout with his feet, the functional bivisibles are ideal. When you continually cast a long line, a high-riding fly is essential. Ray, on the other hand, fishes a short line, and spends most of his time in flat water where the trout have plenty of time to examine his offerings—this is how and where exact imitation pays off. Lee, the one-fly wonder, fishes hard all day long, and it seems to me that he takes trout by sheer casting power. He literally smothers a river with his Leadwing, and the law of averages works in his favor. Keep your fly on the water ninety per cent of the day and you have to catch fish. The Leadwing has always been a good pattern on the Broadhead, Beaverkill, Ausable, and other Eastern rivers, so Lee becomes an efficient angler with the very minimum of fly patterns. I won't pretend that these analyses are complete, they simply indicate why we have so many schools of thought, and why you can't be dogmatic about fly patterns. The contents of a fly box are governed by what a man fishes for, where he fishes, how he casts, the length of his experience, and the size of his bank account.

The history of the dry fly goes back to over one hundred years, and more than likely somebody had floated a fly a century before that. Pulman mentions the floater in *Vade Mecum of Fly Fishing for Trout* in 1841, and James Wallwork, author of *The Modern Angler* (vintage 1847) tells us that "if you angle in quick running waters, your fly must always swim on top under the continual inspection of your eye." It is noticeable, too, that Wallwork favored the use of four patterns: the Red, Green, Black, and Gray Palmers. Judging from the observation about the eye and knowing the silhouette of palmer-tied flies, Wallwork was of the functional school and wasn't too concerned with imitation.

When you consider the variety of water types covered in one day of angling, fast and slow, glassy and broken, shallow and deep, the reasons for success or the lack of it should be fairly obvious. Suppose you start the day in flat water, casting to rising fish with a small, sparsely tied Brown Spider—not the long spade hackle variety but medium legged. The spider will sit down with a minimum of disturbance and is not likely to alarm the trout. It's reasonable to assume that under normal conditions you'll get a share of fish. Considering the trout for what he is—an emotionless creature, so removed in the chain of evolution that he can't even burp—it hardly seems logical that he'd pass up food. Through his lidless eyes he probably sees pinpoints of light made by the spider's hackles, the same delicate impressions made by the legs of a mayfly. To speculate further only invites complications.

Now, move upstream into fast water and meet a new problem. Here the trout is probably looking for a wavering, blurred image shifting on the surface—he's lying close to the bottom, out of the full head of current, and the delicate silhouette of a spider dry is hardly sufficient to bring him up. What's more, the spider doesn't float well in swift water, and you find yourself fishing "blind." Changing to a bushy bivisible will probably do the trick as both of you can see it.

Later in the day you will wade into a long riffle, but there's little insect activity and nothing rising. This calls for a medium dressing, something between a spider and a bivisible—say a Light Cahill. This pattern has more bulk than the spider but is arranged in a more natural insect form than the bivisible. If your eyes are keen, or if you fish a short line, the Cahill wouldn't even need wings, but considering the durability of mallard flank feather, the wings on a Cahill will help spot the fly in overhead afternoon light. If the light is glaring toward you, the Dark Cahill might be in order. Pattern is not of great importance because you are searching the riffle, and all you need is a fly that floats properly —offering a lifelike mouthful to the fish. If, in the course of your search, a big trout starts tipping up, there's time enough to change to a sparser dressing—from a smooth bore to a rifle, once you have a stationary target.

It is generally accepted that an angler can get along with four or five different fly patterns and catch trout anywhere. You can do a very competent job with an Adams Quill, a Light Cahill, Brown Bivisible and a Royal Coachman (hairwing), for instance, provided the fly behaves like an insect after you throw it on the water. The dancing mayfly drifts gracefully; the clumsy caddis fly bewildered by his long feelers flops about in perpetual motion; the flying ants, clouds of them fall to the water in the slightest breeze and drift for a few yards. At the first pressure of current they submerge. Here is a form and a drift that few men learn to imitate—the half floating, half-sunken path of the natural. Yet, a Brown Bivisible with its hackle trimmed close to the hook shank will work wonders. In short, the dry fly angler must suggest form and motion with feathers and steel.

There are a number of fly patterns, well known to the fishing trade, which get results of a sort almost every day of the season, provided the angler covers enough water. The Quill Gordon, Cahill, March Brown, and Royal Coachman are good examples. It would have to be a mighty poor day when one of these patterns wouldn't bring up at least a few fish in a mile of river. This is a pure case of catching the trout that want to be caught, not necessarily the trout you want to catch. I will not linger now over difficult trout or odd flies that I have caught them on, as the conclusions would not be especially valuable. The chances of circumstances being repeated are remote, and this chapter would be likened to a system of beating roulette. Emphasis should be put on suiting the fly to the water. I think this not only simplifies dry fly work, but washes away 85 per cent of the more abstract musing that confuses anglers—who want to improve their skill.

The most practical solution I have found to the pattern question, is to divide my flies into three groups, just as the water types were divided. The first group for casting over rising fish in open water demands that the impact of the falling fly must be light. The pattern must be a reasonable insect imitation or the merest suggestion of insect life, such as the spider type fly. Casting will be from short to medium ranges, and consequently floating power is not the chief consideration. A size 14 hook would be average, with some No. 12's where the fish run large and No. 16's for low, glassy water. My personal choice would be a Cream, or Badger Spider with gold tinsel body, a Coch-y-bondhu Spider with gold tinsel body, a Blue Dun Spider with an unstripped condor quill body—these will work in any stream —a Quill Gordon, small and lead-colored, an English March Brown, and a Whirling Blue Dun.

Both the March Brown and the Whirling Blue Dun have upright style divided wings, which brings us to a rather important consideration. I have never found the upright, made from the primary wing feathers of some bird, wholly practical. Patterns such as the Coachman, Black Gnat, and Ginger Quill proved to be a nuisance, as the pretty little wings quickly tore apart and flapped in the breeze. Instead of the fly "cocking" after the first few floats, it merely relaxed on the surface as if the jig were up. The wings soaked up water and caused the fly to spin in the air. Without a rising fish to work over, the upright was of little real value. For a number of years I depended on the V-shaped white feathers of a Coachman to follow my cast at dusk. Then came the development of hairwing flies, and I found a substitute in the cocked strands of white calf tail for the Coachman. Harry Darbee introduced the White Winged Black Gnat with its white hackle point wings and clipped caribou hair body; the old chenille-bodied Gnat soaked up water like a sponge. Experience indicated that a spentwing Ginger Quill was as good, if not better, than the usual divided wing, and thus I emptied my box gradually of divided-wing flies. The reason I have not eliminated the March Brown and the Whirling Blue Dun even though they have divided wings is simply because I have not found substitutes that work as well.

In glassy water, when large trout are bubbling at the surface, a spider or variant generally takes fish. There are times when a bunched-wing fly, like the Quill Gordon, will do a little better, and there are still other times late in the day when a small, but heavier dressing will bring good results. Neither the March Brown nor Whirling Blue Dun imitate anything in particular. I realize that there are naturals called by both names, but there is such a great variety of them that it's hardly worth the effort to be specific. The March Brown tied with long partridge hackles and partridge tail wings reminds me more of a small brown moth than the many kinds of mayflies it is said to represent; at any rate, Chetham wrote of the "Moorish Brown" in 1681, and its popularity has not diminished. The Whirling Blue Dun was described by Izaak Walton in 1654, and dressed with its proper ginger hackle and gray muskrat fur body, it is as good today as it was then.

The second group of flies is for fast, broken water—patterns that are strictly functional which float like a cork and attract fish. A size 12 hook is about average, but a few No. 10 and No. 14 dressings should be included for heavy and thin water conditions. A representative half-dozen might include the Brown, Black, and Badger Bivisible, a Royal Coachman with hairwing, Irresistible, and Gray Wulff. Floatability is not only an important consideration in fast water fishing but a real problem on moving water at sundown and thereafter. By then your line is soggy, your wrist and hand are tired, and if everything is running normally, the best fish of the day are feeding. Changing to a fresh fly in the dusk is time-consuming, and even if you do bend a new one on, the next fish will probably slime the hackles. Don Martinez of West Yellowstone, Montana, came up with a practical solution several years ago in designing a series of rough-water flies which I have used with some success on Eastern waters. Don summed up the problem in a letter several years ago:

Night after night last summer on the lower Madison I kept wishing to heaven I had a fly that would really float and that I could see right up till full dark. We caught fish, quite a lot of big ones, in fact, but most of them were hooked accidentally, frequently when the fly had sunk and gone on down stream below me. The fish just happened to pull against the inertia of the line in the water and hooked himself.

Well, anyway, I made up some flies with clipped caribou hair bodies along the lines of the Irresistible (Rat-face MacDougalls) but made the bodies oversize so that the air held in the spongy hair offset the weight of the hook and made a positive floater. That is to say, the specific gravity of the fly is less than water. At this point we are a little ahead of the Irresistibles and other flies made with the clipped hair body but only to the extent of somewhat better floating qualities due to the oversize hair body.

Of course a fly with a bulky body looks clumsy and I didn't think they'd work on large, smart fish in clear, shallow water. Specifically, I thought they'd be worthless in the Firehole and in Flat Creek at Jackson, Wyoming. In these two streams you have chalk stream conditions, large trout in thin, slow-moving water. In past years we always used 16's and 18's, very lightly dressed. You are casting to rising fish altogether and you either get them on the first or rarely the second or third cast, or you don't get them at all and go on to a new fish. Anyway, these bulky flies not only worked fully as well as the slim-bodied affairs we'd always used in the past; they worked even better. Maybe because they float clear up mostly out of the water they suggest life to the fish, but no use speculating about the ways of trout.

So far there is nothing very new or sensational but in my dim-witted way I kept thinking about how swell it would be if I could work out a fly that would float right on top of the water and continue to float that way hour after hour. Although these caribou bodied flies float like any other fly, they get water-logged, and once soaked they stay wet for a long time and do not respond to reoiling. The reason being that when the cells of the porous hair get filled up with water they are like those old hollow lines we got a few years back, when wet they were really wet, and they stayed wet. You could squeeze the lines and milk the water out of them, but it got right back in again. The caribou flies without any treatment other than the usual dressing with Mucilin were an improvement but only a partial solution. What was needed was something to seal the air into the hair and it looks as though I've stumbled on to the answer.

For years I've been putting clear top dressing on station wagon tops after the original coating on the fabric wears thin and starts to leak. This stuff is put out by Du Pont and a very similar—identical, I think—preparation is sold by Firestone auto stores. Anyway, the stuff is intended for fabric auto tops as on convertibles. It stands up for months on end even when the car sits out in the baking sun all day; lasts several months in fact. I figured it might work on flies for a pre-dressing and applied it a day or so before use to allow time for the stuff to dry off. Unfortunately, it leaves a waxy residue and tends to gum the hackles of conventional flies, making them unsightly. On the new "rough-water" flies this doesn't matter.

The third group is for flat, open water, when searching for fish with no apparent hatch on the stream. Of the six patterns, five are bunched-wing flies, and one is a spentwing. They are not as lightly dressed as the first group, nor as heavily dressed as the second. They have an orthodox mayfly form and are seen easily at long distances. A size 12 hook is about average for searching-flies, but a few No. 14's should be included for low water conditions or when the prevailing hatches have been of small insects. On my streams the best patterns have been the Light and Dark Cahill, Adams Quill, Hendrickson, and Gray Fox.

I realize that listing fly patterns in this offhand fashion is almost heresy. For Midwestern fishing, especially in Michigan, Wisconsin and Minnesota, I would have Helen Shaw tie up the Kade version of the Royal Coachman and the Michigan Hopper.

The Western angler will want a Blue Upright, a Red Upright, hairwing caddis imitations, maybe a Truckee Silver, and mostly flies tied on No. 10 hooks. The Canadian angler will want more "flash"—a Montreal, Silver Doctor, and others wearing bright snips of tinsel. These alterations might add some stature to the list given—or maybe they just add the essential ingredient of confidence one needs in putting a fly in front of a trout. At any rate, the local equivalent of the flies I suggested is good enough —as long as you have a pattern that floats high in rough streams, one that is durable and lifelike for the searching water, and one that drops like thistledown on a glassy surface. You might add a fly with white wings in case you're going to fish at dusk.

The size of a fly has a great deal to do with the taking of trout. It is safe to say that the angler can get along with a No. 12 for general purposes. If the prevailing wind conditions cause the fly to be delivered crudely, it may be necessary to change to a larger or smaller size to maintain some delicacy in the cast. The trout, of course, is the final judge, but generally you can work out a compromise.

I waded into the railroad side of the Cemetery Pool one June morning and began the slow grind upstream. This part of the Beaverkill has never been good to me. I've taken very few fish from it, so consequently I find it a logical place to start a morning's fishing. By the time I've worked to the pocket water above, where a good fish may be lying, my casting has lost its sleepy rhythm. On this particular morning, I could hardly get halfway through the pool; every other cast brought a strike and I missed fish after fish. It seemed as if they did nothing but nip at the tail of the fly.

The pattern happened to be a Hendrickson. I accepted the improbable and changed to a Dark Cahill. The same thing happened again. A trout would rise and do nothing but bump his nose against the hook, lifting the fly a fraction of an inch off the surface. I changed to several other patterns and finally decided the size was wrong. A Light Cahill happened to be the first small fly I tried, a No. 16, and after taking a few fish on it I changed to a No. 16 Dark Cahill. That worked too. I changed flies a dozen times over, and by the time I reached the pocket water at least twenty trout had been hooked and released.

Many similar experiences come to mind in which size played a major role. Sometimes it is impossible to tell just why it did. It can happen when there are no naturals on the water, and it can happen when certain naturals are; contrary to the match-the-hatch rule there have been occasions in my experience, and that of others, when an artificial *smaller* than the natural was the only taking fly. There is room for much speculation, but lacking the trout's point of view, the angler might simply play safe and carry a variety of sizes. This is much more important than a variety of patterns.

It would be short-sighted to say that an imitationist doesn't have his feet on rock bottom. In many cases the popularity of some local fly pattern is due to the fact that it is used more than any other pattern. However, in every section of the country, on every stream, you will find some fly that the trout take more freely than others. Most of these flies imitate some local form of bug life which appears in such numbers that it becomes important to both the trout and the angler.

In many Western states a stonefly imitation is considered essential at certain times of the year, while in the Midwest and Eastern states the green drake demands a pattern. I have witnessed stonefly hatches that were so heavy that the angler literally breathed them, and green drake hatches of such intensity that nearby roads became slippery from the bodies of insects when clouds of them piled into street lamps and automobiles. Other insect forms, the flying ant, beetles, the night-hatching elophila moth, and the grannom (shad fly), to name a few, may cover the river like a blanket of snow for short periods of time, and the imitationist has a field day.

Once the annual hatch of grannoms is gone, however, trout change their feeding habits and move out of the flats into fast water. The low sparse silhouette of a shad fly imitation—so deadly in flat water—floats miserably on a broken surface. For all practical purposes the pattern can be put aside until next season, and the angler can go back to his functional patterns. Normally, the air will be full of insects, mayflies and caddis flies, beetles, grasshoppers, crickets, and whatnot. What rule of priority makes the mayfly more important than the beetle, or the caddis more charming than the cricket? If you examine a trout's stomach it will be evident that whatever the air is full of, the trout is full of. Fish are like vacuum cleaners working on a stone floor and a liquid ceiling.

Many beginners labor under the delusion that some recondite knowledge is required for success, so they disregard the more pressing problems of leader, line, and hand. The chronic fly changer is invariably troubled with his casting tools but prefers wrestling with a less realistic problem of the precise color in a Quill Gordon's hackle. This is a chain reaction from the day when the air was full of Quill Gordons, and Mr. Fly Changer cast a very bad line indeed. In fact, if he had the *real* fly on his hook, the results would be no different. How deep one should dig into the pattern question is, as I pointed out earlier, subject to the other skills and attitudes developed by the individual.

There have been countless experiments performed on the vision of fish and their response to certain colors—and there has been a vast number of books written projecting both founded and fanciful theories. Most of it has been good groundwork, but in the majority of cases a practical, unbiased application was never attempted in the field. In 1947 the Laboratory of Limnology and Fisheries at Cornell University cooperated in some experiments which gave a group of local fly-tiers a chance to test their flies under rigid and impartial experimental conditions. The flies were fished in a definite area by a number of anglers on successive days, for specified periods of time, and the result was that under the conditions of the experiment, no pattern superiority was apparent. This experiment seems to indicate that fly-fishing is not so complicated after all.

In 1857, W. C. Stewart wrote in *The Practical Angler*, "The great error of fly fishing is that the angler fishes downstream whereas he should fish up." To the anglers of Scotland, where Stewart then held a timorous rank as authority, the upstream direction was pure heresy. It was not that earlier fly-fishers hadn't slapped a belt of flies upriver on occasion—the audacity of the man was in recommending it as habitual practice. But Stewart's book was reprinted many times during the next seventy years. His thesis, that in upstream fishing the angler is not easily seen by the trout, that the water is undisturbed, and that the fish is hooked more easily, became a classic for the nebulous school of dry fly angling. By the time Samuel Camp was ready to produce *Fishing With Floating Flies* in 1913, the New World had accepted these upstream concepts to be as inviolable as the law of gravity. To quote Camp:

> I believe that printed briefs for or against up or down stream fishing with the fly are wearisome to the average well-read and experienced angler; wherefore brevity in discussing this point seems advisable. As regards wet fly fishing any broad-minded angler willingly concedes that under certain conditions it is best to fish the stream up and under other conditions to fish down. The dry fly man, however, has no option in the matter; regardless of all other factors for upstream fishing, the practical fact remains that the floating fly *cannot* [Italics mine—A. J. McC.] be fished downstream for when thus cast it is drowned almost at once. [1]

While Mr. Camp was perfectly correct in turning anglers around, other angling authorities of the day had little or no use for the upstream method. Dr. James A. Henshall, for example,

[1] Camp, Samuel, *Fishing With Floating Flies*, p. 65. New York: The Macmillan Co., 1913. Used with permission of the publishers.

expressed the opinion that dry fly fishing would never become popular in this country—not a particularly accurate forecast—because "for one reason, that the dry fly must be cast upstream, which will never be a favorite method with American anglers."

One bright June morning, many years ago, I was fishing the Big Delaware with Dan Todd. It was the first time I ever saw Long Eddy, a wild sweep of bubbling water about two hundred yards wide. With cool equanimity Dan knocked all traditions in a cocked hat. I watched him cast for at least an hour. His line sped out, and then the bushy gray fly bounced downstream where it simply hung in the current. Sometimes a trout would rap the fly while it was moving; other times a big brown boiled to the surface while the fly was anchored against a tight line. But most of the fish hit when he skittered the fly back. Here was a disrespectful soul making random downstream casts, taking brown trout in weights from two to four pounds. Ever since that day on Long Eddy, I have been turning around once in awhile, and the results were most profitable.

At times drag can be put to good advantage. Drag in case you are not acquainted with it, is that condition which causes a dry fly to kick up a little wake and go skimming across the surface. The fly gets its speed from the line which is caught in faster currents, thus pulling the fly along. This is seldom attractive to a trout. As a matter of fact, a dragging fly and line will generally send the fish diving for cover. So the dry-fly fisherman casts his feathers upstream, putting enough slack in the cast to get a natural drift. With the line floating back toward the angler, he can make the necessary adjustments with his rod to keep the line from bellying in the current. If he were to face downstream and cast, the line would tighten up almost immediately. This is so difficult to prevent that few people ever turn around.

We know, too, that trout always rest with their heads facing upstream; consequently, the easiest way to stalk them is by facing the same direction and coming up from behind. The angler can get nearer his quarry, hook it more easily, and play it in water that has already been covered. With this weight in favor of upstream casting, dry fly fishing is resolved to a simple formula. Yet the dry fly downstream can be a deadly method at times, and if executed properly, will take large trout from spots that would otherwise go untouched.

Late one afternoon, on the Willowemoc River, I waded into a stretch of water that squeezed between high, brush-covered banks. At the head of the riffle, a string of piano-sized boulders straddled the stream bed, so I began by testing the deep pockets around each rock. On the far bank, a dark eddy swept in behind one boulder, and above this bare dome a fat hemlock dropped a screen of branches to the water, blocking off any casts from a downstream or across-stream position. I walked a short distance above the eddy to where a gravel bar sloped out into the river and by wading carefully, I managed to flip a bucktail into the quiet parts around the hemlock sweeper. It was like casting into a tunnel. On the first toss, a trout flashed behind the fly. On the second cast he moved away from the fly and took a position over a patch of white pebbles next to the boulder.

I tried a smaller bucktail on the next cast, and then a wet fly which succeeded only in flushing a small brook trout. The native came speeding straight upstream and wiggled under a rock almost at my feet. Nothing seemed to interest or disturb the fat brown trout lying next to the boulder. He rested there, his white mouth opening and closing. I didn't bother to cast anymore, but instead sat on a half submerged log wondering what to do next. The idea of floating a dry fly over him occurred to me, but it took the trout to lend encouragement.

I saw the fish rise about forty feet below me; his sharp head broke the surface and slid gently out of sight. I worked out my cast until there was just enough line to fall five or six feet short of his position, and then, with an abrupt check, the bivisible fell to the water and drifted slowly over his lair. The trout crossed the patch of white pebbles and moved slowly behind the fly. Several times he made feeble passes at it, never quite making up his mind. Time was running out. I kept lengthening the drift with slack, but now the fly began moving faster toward the tail of the eddy and suddenly the fish turned, facing upstream. I stopped the slack and raised my rod tip, skidding the bivisible right back over his head. That movement of the fly was like touching off a shotgun. The trout took the fly instantly, and made a surface churning run straight downstream. Had the fish been less ambitious, a few turns around the hemlock branches would have been an easy out.

After netting the fish I walked back up to the hemlock and spent a few minutes examining the branches. It was no surprise to find three different pieces of leader hanging there. In all probability the sweeper was good for thirty more. On a hard-fished Catskill stream, you don't find sizable trout in places that are easily covered. This lair was probably by-passed a hundred times in the course of a season.

The parachute cast is the best way to drop a fly downstream. Line and leader will stretch out and fall slack—just slack enough to give you a long drift without paying out too much line. Most important, is that the slack is not concentrated in one big belly of line—but is *distributed* throughout its floating length. When slack is concentrated in one area, too much line is exposed broadside to the current, and drag starts almost immediately. If you want to reach a fish that is out of range, make a cast downstream, and by shaking line out, the weight of the floating slack will carry the fly out. The parachute cast is useful not only downstream, but across currents of varying speeds as well.

To execute the parachute cast, you false cast in the ordinary manner, holding the rod and line higher than usual until the required length is obtained on the last cast. On the forward drive, stop the rod at *vertical*, simultaneously lowering the rod hand about 18 inches; this abrupt stop will pull the leader and

line back, while the lowering of the rod drops it to the water in
the same position as it was checked. This differs from the ordinary slack line cast in which the angler lengthens his line until
it extends a few feet beyond the target—at which point he checks

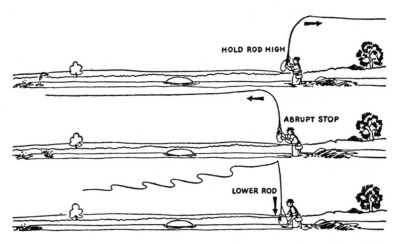

Figure 12. To make the parachute cast, you false-cast in the usual
manner but holding your rod a little high. The reel should be level
with your eyes. When the desired length of line is extended, stop
the rod at vertical, simultaneously lowering your rod hand about
18 inches. This differs from the ordinary slack line cast in which
the angler stops the rod and lowers the tip instead of his hand.

the forward cast, simultaneously lowering his rod *tip*. The result
is wide elbows of slack which are difficult to control.

For downstream casting I like to use small, stiff hackled bivisibles. They not only float well, but on a calm surface their wake
is hardly noticeable. A heavy hackled fly is apt to kick up too
much disturbance and put the fish down. I don't think pattern

means a thing in this type of fishing. A gray, black, or brown bivisible—depending on which you can see the best—will bring a trout to the top if he's going to come at all. Flies tied with a wide hackle at the eye skip over the water better than those bivisibles of almost uniform diameter, which, unfortunately, are in the majority. The longer hackle at the eye causes the fly to tip forward, keeping the hook in the air. After a little experimentation you'll find quite a difference in the working qualities of various designs.

There's a subtle distinction between a "worked" fly and dragging fly. To clear this up: a worked fly is one that is moving (in this case, on the surface) against the current in short, pulsing strokes, bearing a fleeting resemblance to some strong-winged insect that wants to go upstream. On the other hand, a dragging fly is less artfully played, and the lure makes a broad wake that frightens the trout. Why one man can work his lure and the other can only drag it is as elusive as why one man can paint and the other cannot. Judging from the anglers I have watched who can bring a husky brown trout boiling into a worked floater, I would say a highly-developed fish sense is essential. I do know that heavy-bellied fly lines and heavy-hooked dry flies are no asset upstream or down. To get the best results the leader should be as long and as light as possible.

The complete downstream technique consists of letting the fly drift on a slack line until you've covered the holding water, and then bringing the fly back upstream in short darting strokes. It's a good idea to make the fly dart with some authority—don't let the feathers hang in the current like a wet mop. The natural drift downstream will give the fish a chance to rise to a slack cast if he's so inclined—but retrieve with a teasing, jumping motion by flexing your wrist and slowly raising the rod tip. If the fish rises and follows the fly while it's drifting freely, keep paying slack out to the very last moment—but if he rejects the fly, stop the drift before the line passes over him. These suggestions are simply common-sense fishing. In any given situation you'll have to adjust the length of drift to the reaction of the fish, provided you see him.

If there's no fish in sight, you'll have to rely on your knowledge of trout habits and cover the holding water as though you knew the fish were there. Such a situation is in the minority, however, as the usual reason for turning around is to cover a fish who wouldn't play ball on the upstream field. On rare occasions you might want to try a complete reverse when things are slow, and in that event simply follow the drift-and-work routine, making a minimum of casts and working each for a maximum time on the water.

Several years ago, on the upper Campbell River, I fished down through a stretch of rough water which tumbled over a small fall into a broad, flat pool. It had been perfect wet fly water up to this point, but the trout were uniformly small, a condition not uncommon in isolated sections of bedrock rivers. Trout food can't thrive on bare, current-swept rock. But this giant basin of clear water had a good gravel bottom and as I expected, cutthroats were showing at the surface. I walked along the shore studying the gravel bars that sloped into the river. One bar, which dipped off a small island, bisected most of the pool so I waded out thirty or forty yards and stopped for a cigarette. The water was so clear that every stone sparkled like a jewel. Three of four fish were working out of range, but just before I finished my smoke they had drifted into reach.

In the wilderness of Vancouver Island you wouldn't expect a trout to be suspicious. These trout were not suspicious—they were downright incredulous. The larger fish foraged by himself, tipping up and down, sucking in caddis flies as the slow current drifted him along. My casts were beautiful. The little fly sat quietly on the water and drifted almost into the trout's mouth time and again, but the fish just ignored it. I covered the smaller trout just as neatly and got the same response. It wasn't until the trio had drifted downstream from me that the fun began.

The first parachute cast didn't get a glance on the slack drift, but a few twitches on the dragging fly brought the big cutthroat roaring into the feathers. There began one of the busiest day's fishing I've ever had. Bill MacDonald, Fishing Editor of *Forest and Outdoors,* joined me later that afternoon, and between the two of us we landed an estimated sixty trout up to four pounds in weight.

Black bass and Atlantic salmon will both hit a worked dry fly. As a matter of fact, they will both hit a dragging dry fly as often as not; consequently, there's no novelty fishing them downstream. Trout are more cautious feeders, however; the brook trout less than the rainbow, and the rainbow less than the brown. This difference within the trout family has been proved time and again in controlled scientific research projects. I cite this in passing simply to point out that statistics seem to bear out the attitude of each trout species in taking a fly fished in any manner.

There are definitely times when a "worked" dry fly will take trout while the orthodox upstream, drag-free cast will not. I've paid particular attention to this in my trout fishing in recent years. Probably the best period is in late season. The New York trout season closes in September, and usually during the last days when our weather is neither summer nor fall, stream fishing is poor. I have found, however, that the dry fly worked downstream will make a respectable showing when dead leaves and wind-borne seeds drift with the river. Gone are the fat hatches of insects that brought trout to feeding; beetles, shrimps, snails, and odd land flies provide an occasional meal to these whimsical fish. One would expect a period of heavy eating before cold weather sets in, but such has never been the case in my experience. The trout become most difficult. Yet a cross and downstream cast left to float and then drawn back jerkily often produces amazing catches when an orthodox upstream cast fails.

Like most other anglers, my downstream dry fly fishing for years had been more of an emergency measure than a technique. We know, of course, that on many white water Western rivers, downstream dry fly fishing is the *only* technique. The boiling riffles of the McKenzie in Oregon, for instance, are traditionally fished downstream. A large, bushy dry fly is tossed in likely places and skipped back over the surface—without even bothering to cover the water with a slack drift first. The surface is so broken that drag doesn't matter in the least. This same technique isn't as successful in flat water, or in Midwestern and Eastern rivers where brown trout predominate. But the parachute cast seems to satisfy a good percentage of the flat water fish, and I think the reason is fairly obvious. Assuming that the slack drift rides over a trout without showing any line, it's reasonable to allow that some interest was aroused in this "natural" float—and when the fly does come to life, by darting against the current, our victim (who has had his eye on it) responds with little suspicion. This is a far cry from slapping a cast out that drags over the fish from the moment it hits the water.

I think the most convincing incident occurred on the upper Housatonic River in Connecticut last August. The Meadows is restricted to fly-fishing only; consequently, some walloping big brown trout live in that broad water. A daily rise and fall in water level due to the opening and closing of the dam allows just a few fishing hours in the evening. Trout were dimpling the surface all around me, and the best I could manage was one smallish brownie during the first hour. A long, black fish lay in a riffle, making those head and tail rises that mark the wise one. Determined to do him in, I cast and cast, stopping only to change flies. Once I looked over my shoulder to check a sloppy back cast and saw a trout just as heavy as the first one—going through the same motions. In an instant I did an about-face, and shortened my line, parachuting a cast right down his alley. The trout actually came to the drift and turned away, but when the fly started to dart over him he pulled it under the surface with a strong tug. There was just enough light left to go back and try for the other fish, and the worked fly succeeded again.

You cannot reasonably expect to get your best dry fly fishing by fishing downstream every day. For the many reasons pointed out earlier in this chapter, casting upstream is certainly most effective. However, the parachute cast is of infinite value over rising trout and for covering water that cannot be reached from a downstream position. On days when nothing seems to be moving fish, it certainly pays to reverse the field and stir them up —even on placid chalk streams, where a moving fly has brought smashing strikes. Remember, until the year 1846 it was considered heresy to cast upstream, and in the transition to dry fly fishing during the years following, none but the dour wet fly fisherman continued to wade with the current. I think much of the dry fly art was lost by this one-track mindedness.

Fishing the dry fly downstream is an accepted practice now and has been brought full cycle by Leonard Wright's book *Fishing the Dry Fly as a Living Insect* (1972). That's what I had in mind only Wright said it better. In terms of modern-day tackle a No. 3 or No. 4 double-taper line and the longest rod that will handle these sizes, which is about 8 feet, is the ideal for downstream fishing. If the line is too heavy it will drag the fly under and if the rod is too short you lose control of the float rather quickly. Theoretically, one should have a 9-foot rod of about 2

ounces in weight which may be possible in the new
high-modulus graphite material; this would minimize the
length of line on the surface—a tremendous advantage
upstream or down.

Back in 1939 I wrote an article for *Outdoor Life*
("Bouncing for Trout") in which I described the use of
the then popular silk-bait casting line, and alternately,
dental floss as a "fly line." This could only be accomplished
on a downstream wind and was strictly an experiment.
Nevertheless under the right conditions the results were
phenomenal in terms of moving fish, as the line remained
airborne most of the time while a big spider dry bounced
over the surface. I can hardly recommend this as a fishing
method, but with the constantly evolving refinements in
tackle the day may come when superfine equipment is
available.

CHAPTER VIII

Stiff Hackles and Soft

THERE IS one fly that a beginner or an expert can use with complete confidence on most fishing days. I passed over it briefly in the last chapter in order to keep my general theory in perspective. Lest you suspect me of whimsy, I want to reaffirm the fact that you can do an excellent job on any stream with four types of dry flies—a bivisible, a spider, a bunched wing pattern, and a fly with white wings. Of these four, the spider-type fly is most interesting. When the elaborate clockwork of insect hatches comes to life you will have difficult hours with wise fish; they can trap you into antique, useless habits of thinking. If a feeding trout ignores fly after fly, the thesis of exact imitation might seem valid. However, I doubt seriously that we can imitate exactly any insect with feathers and silks, but we can achieve the right caricature by color, refraction, shape, action, size, or any combination of these qualities. The fact that many, apparently selective trout will fall for a spider when nearly perfect imitations fail is important to remember.

There was a brook trout who lived in a flat pool at the head of our night pasture, just where the stream broke out of a hemlock stand. This fish had a casual innocence in the way he would rest at the very tail of the run, inspecting those flies that I threw at him day after day. I would come from below him, and by hiding in a screen of tall grass, make a thirty or thirty-five foot cast that put the fly directly in his line of vision. In all fairness to my trout, he did strike on two different occasions and I missed both. But as the summer passed he became more and more indifferent. Apparently this brookie spent his whole day in exactly the same place, because I would find him there nearly every time I went out. My trouble was in avoiding drag. The fly would float a few feet, and at the instant my trout would start for it, the fly would kick up a little wake, sending him scurrying across the pool and under a boulder. As any angler knows, a situation like this can become an obsession.

Late one afternoon I found my problem fish in his regular position, so I tied on a Cream Spider and wished it well. The fly settled easily and came dancing downstream, while the line, caught in faster currents nearby, started to race out of control. I gave some slack, but in that fraction of a second drag was inevitable—the belly of the line pulled at the fly. Spiders, however, are not ordinary flies. Instead of skimming through the surface, the fly spun and bounced off the water in a startling broad jump, and my trout was fastened to the hook. I would like to pause and reflect on what followed, but the brookie did little more than thrash about, arriving at my net with the passive dignity of a spent champion.

If you were to fish every day during that period of the year when trout rise to floating flies—using a spider or variant—you would catch your daily share of trout and probably hook some of the largest ones that will ever come to any dry fly. I won't even make exceptions about where you do this fishing. Provided it is water with a normal fly-eating trout population, you are going to get a chance at every fish who wants to be caught and even a few who usually know better. The only qualification is that you have a reasonable aptitude for casting. Your observer bows to all rebukes he is going to get for this epilogue, but I'll allow no shoddy substitutions on the end of my leader. The case of the Spider is in point, and I record it even though we are spying on the weakness of trout.

Of all trout flies, the one you can least afford to be without is the spider. It can be a Brown Spider, a Badger Spider, a Blue

Dun Spider, or whatever kind you like, but at least one of these high riding floaters should be in the kit of every serious fly fisherman. The spider is thought to imitate long-legged insects like the crane fly, spider, or water strider. True or not, they seem to suggest insect life in general because they are usually effective even when caddis flies, midges, and mayflies are on the water. In appearance, the spider-type dry fly consists of a relatively small hook tied with extra large hackle. Although they are sometimes made without bodies or tails, in my experience a fly so tied is much less effective. When the spider is tied with a tiny pair of wings it is properly called a "variant," but in recent years the terms have become arbitrary, and many variant patterns are now wingless. The great attraction of this fly is its ethereal, almost lifelike ability to dance across the surface. It will even turn around on the water, and the slightest change in current or puff of wind will send it skating for a few inches before floating again. The secret of course, is in the hackle, which may be two inches or more in diameter, depending on the hook size. Hook and hackle are out of proportion to each other, the hackle being roughly three or more times greater than the hook would regularly require in an ordinary dry fly.

The reactions of trout to a spider-type fly are different from their responses toward ordinary flies. Logical behaviour among trout is nothing more than a pleasant myth at best; the spider, for instance, commonly causes the fish to rise above the surface and take the fly going down. Now whether this is because the fly actually excites them, or because the sensitive movement of a spider simulates an active insect about to take off, I am not sure. I have caught many trout this way, and over a long period of time the only impression left me is that the fish were anxious that the fly should not escape.

I found a brown trout on the Willowemoc below Harry Darbee's place last summer. The fish was rising in a length of bouncy water between two pools, and after I tried several casts with a

Cahill he stopped his feeding. For a moment he drifted backward with the current, sinking very slowly, but when the fly didn't come down again as he expected, we both felt relieved. A minute passed and he was back at the surface. Quite obviously, I had him on guard, and the next cast would be my last chance. I took off the Cahill and knotted on a small Blue Dun Spider; the safest way to try any trout is to suggest an insect form, showing him little to find fault with. Don't mistake this scrap of learning for scholarship—it is an axiom on which fly fishing rests—and you can do with it as you please. I cast the spider so that it fell several yards above his station, and even as the fly floated I knew the trout would take. My Blue Dun rode jauntily over the water, standing on the tips of its hackles. The trout dashed directly at the fly, and then jumped clear of the surface, snatching the spider as he came down. Here was an otherwise reluctant fish suddenly inspired to be an acrobat. Unusual? Not in the least.

The spider-type dry fly is strictly an American innovation. On foreign waters the term "spider" means a long-hackled wet fly, and I point this out because many tackle shops stock the imported kind which are not the same thing. I've often wondered how the chalk-stream fly fisher overlooked the possibility of a long-hackled floater in his still-water casting. The spider really excels on glassy streams. In very fast and broken water a rough, hair-bodied fly or a bivisible would be more effective, as it requires a sizable mouthful to tempt a trout to the top. But in slower places the sparse, free-floating spider leaves nothing to be desired. I use three patterns almost exclusively: a Cream Spider with gold tinsel body, a Coch-y-bondhu Spider with gold body, and a Blue Dun Spider with a condor quill body. These represent the three major insect colorations—cream, brown, and blue-gray. I also have quite a number tied with mixed hackles, grizzly and brown, grizzly and ginger, furnace and ginger, and these work equally as well. The important thing to remember is that the hackle must be stiff, long, and sparse so that the overall effect is no more than a suggestion of insect life. You can't achieve this impression with webby neck hackle. A proper spider is made from spade hackle—the wide hackle found on a rooster's throat. Sometimes on a game cock skin you'll find saddle hackles that are perfect for making spiders; as a rule, however, they are a bit too short. The hooks I like best are No. 14 and No. 16 short shanks of very light wire, but don't hesitate to try No. 18 or even smaller; I have used them down to No. 20 even on heavy fish. Tom Moore showed me some fantastic fishing one day in the channel between Yellowstone and Shoshone Lakes—using nothing but No. 18's and 20's.

It is interesting to note that the spider dry fly is almost foolproof in presentation. No matter how clumsily you shoot your cast the fly will come delicately to the water—provided you do not use too heavy a leader. As a rule of the thumb, a 9-foot leader tapered to 3X at the point is nearly correct for all light trout lines, and if the tippet section of the leader is 30 inches or longer, you just can't bungle a cast. Spiders will not spin or twist a light leader, and although they have little more air resistance than orthodox dry flies, once the cast is checked they execute a slow, deliberate flight to the surface. Furthermore, the spider is less apt to drag on the water, because a pull on the line will send the fly hopping out of trouble. Remember, this fly cocks on the tips of its long hackles and tail with the hook well above the surface. It can even be cast directly downstream and purposely dragged against the current; if your line is floating high the spider will simply walk upstream. Spiders will not get mashed after a few fish are taken, and most patterns are wingless—a feature which many practical anglers appreciate. In my opinion, wings are important only when greater visibility is needed or when a spent-wing hatch is on the surface. Spent-wing flies are in a more limited fashion just as unique as the spider. Speaking of being unique, that reminds me of a day on one of our northern New York trout streams.

A storm started to move over West Canada Creek one afternoon, and as high winds blew up river, the trout began rising in a strong ripple near the far bank. Pale colored duns were hatching in numbers, but as the wind grew, they skidded and skated on the surface, at times even being blown directly upstream. The fish were not taking them evenly—they slashed and jumped at the unpredictable insects. Needless to say the whole performance smacked of spider fishing, and by the time great thunderclaps were overhead, I netted my sixth trout and ran for the car. West Canada is a heavily fished stream, and ordinarily getting a bag of six trout would have been an extremely complex procedure. The point is, that spiders are especially effective on windy days. If you use a long, fine leader, the spider will skate and leap like a frustrated mayfly. Sometimes you'll get the same effect in heavy rivers where the currents conflict but the surface is flat.

The Thompson River is not a trout stream in the usual sense of the word, for the river is deep and in some places over a quarter-mile wide. One is bewildered at first by the currents that merge and run in every direction—marked by streaks of froth which gather in patches of foam that revolve slowly and then dissolve. Floating logs go down in funnel-shaped whirls and reappear later amid hissing air bubbles. I have fished the Thompson for steelhead in its quieter parts around Kamloops and further south in British Columbia, but in the northerly primitive country near Clearwater drainage, there are some remarkable dry fly waters. In one morning, fishing with Don and Sally Carter, we caught and released well over one hundred rainbow trout. They came so easy that we lost interest in catching them.

But on the day I have in mind a school of big rainbows were "making the tour" around a froth-covered pool. The fish were on a spree, yet no splash marked their feeding. A broad tail appeared and disappeared where a trout picked flies out of the foam; then another and another. Sometimes they would swim and rise in a straight line, finally getting on the tops of the long glassy rollers that surged against the rocky shore and then they'd move back out into the main current to make their circuit again. I was fishing with Bill MacDonald, the angling editor of *Forest and Outdoors*. Ordinarily, Bill's fly-rod skill is exceptional, but in two hours of casting we each managed to hook just one small trout. It was difficult fishing; the constant change in direction and length of the cast, frequent fly changing, and steadily rising trout made the perfect background for something miraculous to happen—and it did. Bill tied on a spider, and after a few casts he was fast to a leaping rainbow. Those big rainbows suddenly hit our casts again and again, coming up and over to take the spider on a downward turn. There would be a terribly long pause before the trout took off, and many of them snapped our leaders on the first wild run. As in most of that country, the fish were of a size; while the more abundant Clearwater fish had been two-pounders, our Thompson trout were three-pounders.

Spiders are especially productive in lake fishing. There is one situation in particular, that of high-altitude Western lakes, where midges are the predominant food form; here the spider will frequently take fish who are obviously feeding on insects which seem no larger than the head of a pin. Why this should be, I am not sure, but the spider is a very satisfactory attractor when trout become narrowly wise in their isolation. I was discussing high lake trouting with Frank Dufresne recently, and we discovered that we had identical experiences in widely separated areas. Most people are under the impression that remote trout populations are easy marks—this is not even a fair generalization. Frank pointed out that in the hundreds of mountain lakes he had fished, the greatest majority demanded tiny flies and delicate tackle, and short of actual midge fishing, the spider proved most reliable.

Mile High is a lake formed on a great bed of stones in northern British Columbia. The place Don Carter and I fished that afternoon was a narrow bay where the trout rose merrily, leaping as regular as clockwork. At first glance we thought this was going to be another Clearwater episode, but as the afternoon passed neither one of us had struck a trout, even though we covered one after another. There were many different sedges, midges, and even a few mayflies on the water, and we tried imitating everyone of them. Don took the paddle once more, and we made our third or fourth circuit of the bay. Purely through the process of elimination I arrived finally at the fly-box which held my spiders, and within a very short time we were catching trout. They weren't the biggest fish we saw feeding, but a dozen husky kamloops rainbows came to net. Until this Mile High junket, I had never attached any real significance to spider fishing on mountain lakes. In the light of more recent events I'm fairly well convinced that this is the dry fly man's answer to problem trout at any altitude.

Large trout are not by nature free risers to the dry fly. Big brown trout, especially, stay out of sight and do their feeding at hours when most anglers are sound asleep. Yet, let the green drake or salmon fly hatch by the thousand, and these clouds of temptation clog his brain, halting all rational traffic that a cannibal trout must direct down avenues of safety. Insect food gets out of proportion to his ability to resist it, and for a brief period you and I are in a position to meet the legendary monster. Although a spider could resolve this conflict, there are many kinds and patterns of flies which simulate green drakes and salmon flies —and dozens of them catch trout. But what fly will sometimes bring a hook-jawed brown to the top when there are no great fly hatches or when there is nothing on the water to imitate? I have asked that question of many skilled dry fly men, and the spider was elected by unanimous vote.

I must submit that the facts are not without qualification. In my opinion, the spider dry fly is the best possible attractor in flat or bouncy water; it is a poor floater in swift, broken water where it is not as likely to tempt fish. It is more suggestive of aquatic insect life in general than other types of flies, and the spider stands the best chance of raising large trout if they have any inclination toward surface feeding. But now, before I commit the narrator's crime of implausibility, proceed through the remainder of this chapter knowing that nothing is amiss in our history of plodding truth. I want to point out that there is something to be said for very soft-hackled flies that is generally overlooked.

While fishing in the Blue Ridge Mountains several years ago, Bedell Smith suggested that the Lunn theory of dry fly tying might have a very definite role in our American fishing. We had no opportunity to put the idea in practice; it was just a passing remark made while bass fishing. William Lunn was for many years a river keeper at the Houghton Club on the Test in England. It was his belief that stiff-hackled flies don't "feel" right in the mouth of a trout, nor do they resemble properly an insect in dead calm water where the fish has every chance of inspecting his food. Lunn claimed that a trout would reject a stiff-hackled fly the instant his jaws started to close on it, and from all I've heard of the wise trout living in Houghton water, that may be true.

I didn't attach any significance to the idea immediately, but the more I thought about my random experiences with English-tied dry flies, the more I realized their potential. In the little chalk-stream fishing I have done, my American type dry flies often proved less effective than the softer, sparsely tied patterns made for those waters. Although the hackles curled and looked sloppy, they achieved results on a mirrored surface. Perhaps their flat-bellied posture in floating was more to the trout's liking. Going back over the last twenty years, I can remember many occasions on Eastern streams when these same dry flies brought excellent catches in dead water. The point I am emphasizing of course, is that the soft-hackled fly is associated with slow rising fish in the quietest kind of stream. Such a fly is not for searching or fishing blindly, as it will not float very long. It is for the one-shot caster, the man who can get on a feeding trout without cutting a swath all over the stream.

I have not had time to make serious comparisons between soft hackles and stiff since Bedell and I discussed it that day. It will take many months of dry fly work before anything can be un-covered. At first blush though, there seems to be a kernel of importance here, and possibly our rigid standard of stiff hackle is the most flogged of all whipping-boy hypotheses. After all, there is no one perfect dry fly.

Well, I guess this *has* been flogged because we are back to hackless dry flies in the year 1975 which is where Dame Juliana Berners left off in 1496. The no-hackle concept was given new meaning by two great trout-stream technicians, Doug Swisher and Carl Richards, in their book *Selective Trout* (1971). Their premise, stated oversimply on my part (you must read the book), is that a fly tied without hackle is more natural looking, particularly to selective trout. And indeed they are right. Under the conditions I fished with Doug one day on Michigan's North Branch of the Au Sable, in silky flowing water with rising fish, he expertly proved his thesis. While there is opinion to the contrary, there is nothing in Berners' ambiguous directions to indicate that flies had hackles, or tails for that matter. And during the next 150 years of angling literature, sparse though it may be, we find no mention of a fly hackled in any form except palmer style (along the length of the body like a Woolly Worm).

Although the genesis of fly making in print goes from
Berners to Mascall (1590), Markham (1614), Barker
(1651), Walton (1653), and so on without inspiration
to Venables (1662) and Chetham (1683), everybody
repeated Berners. Understandably overlooked by owl-eyed
historians was the manuscript of Juan de Begara (1624)
which only surfaced in Madrid in 1958. This incidental to
the inheritance of Doña Victoria Gonzalez del Campo,
and is presently owned by Generalíssimo Franco. Totally
original in its concept, the author provided details on tying
flies according to season (month to month) and dressing
these in a style unknown to England. Essentially these were
all no-hackle spent-wing patterns. *Plus ça change . . .*

CHAPTER IX

How to Cast Beyond Sixty Feet

THE RUN of water I stepped into was fully a hundred feet in width, and the fishy-looking pockets were along the far bank. In fact, the weeds were so thick that the only place to cast a fly was in a foot-wide channel, separated from me by what could have been an acre of weed bed. The water was about hip deep, and past experience indicated that I could wade to within several yards of the channel as long as I stayed in the grass and didn't move around too much. This wasn't the most pleasant way to get at a rising trout, but then, a productive angling situation is seldom easy. Fish get large and sometimes abundant just by staying out of the angler's reach.

Several large trout swam blindly into my legs. I could feel the tap and then the squirming as the fish became oriented in some unseen channel below the weeds. Provided none of these trout headed for the far bank, prospects looked pretty good. About twenty feet from the channel I stopped and waited the duration of a cigarette for the disturbance to settle. A woodpecker thumping an ancient oak took time out to look me over, and then went back to his work. Slightly downstream two small trout were consistently rising against what had once been the foundation of a bridge, probably licking larvae off the coarse cement. While watching their antics I heard the sucking pop of a good fish at close range. A fat brown trout had moved from his sunless tunnel under the bush upstream from me and was now weaving in the feeble current about twenty-five feet away.

I knew what I had to do, but my hand was too nervous to take orders. A small olive dun came waltzing downstream, and his big nose barely marked the surface. The fly disappeared without a ripple. If I live to be a hundred I'll never quite manage to keep my nerves at just the proper level when a good trout shows. Considering how narrow the channel was, there seemed to be only one course to take—to cast a right curve, keeping the line on top of the weeds and causing the leader and fly to swing over the fish without drag. To lay the line directly up the channel was out of the question. Sharp-eyed brown trout are not fish that the line can come straight up on, and still have any real promise of a strike.

The first two casts were beautiful curves, but they turned in the wrong direction. Cautiously flipping the fly back off the weeds, I undershot the next cast and threw a curve that put the fly right on his nose—a bit too hard perhaps. At that precise instant another dun came flitting off the weed bed sailing downstream hardly an inch away from the Cahill. The trout turned slowly, sucked in the olive dun, then disappeared under his bush. But before you leave me stewing in my weeds, there is an afterpiece. The wholesome truth is that an expert doesn't always catch his fish but usually manages to find a way of salvaging the wreck he just made. I submit my second trout which, in your philosophic opinion, should atone for this obvious deficiency.

The second trout appeared as the first one did, but so far upstream that I couldn't really make out if the movement were a trout or the shadow of a passing bird. There was little time to waste, but I could wade no farther. Chara weed was hanging on my suspenders. This twice-told tale will be a brief sketch, however, for the line was set in motion, and soon the loop went bowling through the air. It unrolled slowly to propel the fly in a delicate turn behind an almost invisible nylon. This lacked the detail of planning given the first trout, but later at the post mortem I measured 83 feet of retrieved line, a toss that I've had considerable difficulty in repeating from a wet elbow position.

The trout's play was not remarkable, but the moral, thin as it might be, tells us that catching a fish is not always possible at the popular ranges of thirty to forty feet. Fly fishing, when taken in the sequence of events, is similar to a game of chess; one needs the skill to establish an immediate offense, but one also needs the foresight to cope with a distant turn of the game.

I have never made a cast beyond ninety feet when fly-fishing. The few casts that did see all the oiled silk passing through the guides seldom connected, and those that did get a rise were from fish that I could have done without. I'm sure there are a good many anglers who've taken large fish on extra long throws, but from the practical aspect there's a point of diminishing returns. Under actual angling conditions with the caster almost hip deep in water, using delicate equipment, I think it's safe to say that a long cast is from sixty to eighty feet. This is almost twice the distance of our usual fishing range and is a longer reach than most people realize. Sixty feet is apt to look like eighty, and eighty, well, that's the one hundred foot cast a good many of us have made. Of course, with heavy gear on a steelhead river a talented rod wielder can bat out seventy and eighty foot casts using the heavy lines built for that range. In this chapter how-ever, I want to talk about distance in ordinary fishing terms.

The ideal concept of distance casting is to get the rod at full load within five motions—pick up, lay back, speed forward, speed back, and shoot. If the maximum speed and load aren't felt in the fourth motion, then the caster brings his line hand into stronger play and goes forward and back again, accelerating his line by pulling with his left hand before shooting. It's axiomatic that the longer he keeps his line in the air, the less chance he has of reaching the required speed. The few people who can hang on for seven or more motions have strong arms, perfect rhythm, perfect line-hand control—and are either champions or rod breakers. The few polished distance casters I know that do not have strong arms, do have an extremely long line-hand pull, long enough to slip a dropping back cast into high gear if they lose speed. In a way, casting is like driving a car; when you round a curve you slow down, brake slightly, then touch the accelerator with a cautious toe—the fact that you gain control by increasing the speed at the right moment is a reflex rather than conscious action. So it is with casting. You lift line for the approach, it swings back, and the rod speeds it up. The rod then reaches its deepest bend—which acts as the brake while the line straightens out, and then you accelerate for the forward drive. The acceleration is achieved by pulling the line forward with your left hand at the instant the rod offers its fullest resistance to bending. Line and rod tip should then travel at maximum speed.

To understand the stabilizing influence of your line hand, just take your outfit on the front lawn and swish a few casts back and forth. Make an easy back cast—underpower it purposely— and as the line begins to drop toward the ground, start your forward cast, at the same instant pulling the line smoothly forward with your left hand and watching how the falling line snaps out straight. This is your gear shift. Whip the line forward, and as you start toward the next back cast, pull again with your left hand, smoothly and easy—the line speeds back fast in a high, tight loop. As the line straightens out again, it should tug at the rod slightly, in that instant you can "shoot" a few yards to the rear by letting it slip through your line hand (this cuts out excess false casts with a double-taper), or slide your hand toward the butt ring guide to get more pulling distance for the forward cast. The higher you reach, the longer the pull; the longer the pull, the greater the forward velocity. When you shoot line on your back cast, as the speed decreases and the line starts dropping, accelerate again with your left hand, hitting the line hard with the tip—you are shifting gears once more. Now speed it up, higher, faster, lengthen your pull—feed it out backward and forward, and when the bamboo is really bending, then let 'er rip!

In effect you have just made a double line haul. This was certainly the greatest contribution to casting technique in the last century. Although anglers were long aware that the left hand played an important role in effortless casting, it wasn't until Marvin Hedge introduced the exaggerated motions of the double line haul to tournament casting in 1938 that distance records jumped over the 150-foot mark. The double haul gives a line much greater velocity; it will pull out thirty or forty feet of shooting line—adding that much more to a cast. This is how casting champions make their records and how fishermen in the coastal streams make their really long tosses for steelhead and salmon. Even in trout and bass fishing the angler has occasional need to get out seventy or eighty feet of line, and there's no easier way of doing it. There are nine important phases in the double haul—all of which must be smoothly blended: (1) the line-hand reaches as far forward as possible and begins pulling an instant before the rod hand begins to lift; (2) a split second later, rod hand and line hand are working together; (3) the rod is speeding up now, and the line hand is pulling hard; (4) the line hand stops as the back cast straightens out; this stop consumes just a fraction of a second, blending in with the backward movement of line; (5) the line hand now begins to slide upward with the straightening of the back loop in order to get maximum reaching distance for the next line hand pull; (6) line hand and rod hand are in motion again as the forward cast begins; (7) both hands accelerate their movements; (8) faster; (9) the rod hand follows through while the line hand lets go for the shoot.

This, of course, is just the basic procedure. It will be necessary to repeat the process backward and forward several times until maximum tip and line speed are attained. I find it easy to cast over 100 feet by underpowering the first few false casts until I have the proper length of line extended. What this amounts to is almost swinging the line back and forth, timing it as slowly as possible, and then adding the pull to get speed. Some casters hold their left hand stationary until the right hand puts enough speed and snap into the back cast so that it straightens high in the rear before beginning the haul. Either way, when you stop the rod at a position near one o'clock, bring the left hand up to where the right hand is; the line will have enough momentum at that point to take care of itself. At the instant the straightening is complete, bring the left hand down sharply to the first position (at your side) and the double haul is finished. All these motions have to be blended very smoothly. Remember, in practice you will probably develop your own style. Don't accept anything I have outlined as being the correct way—very few people do these things alike, and you'll have to take advantage of your strongest points—wrist, forearm, timing, or whatever the case might be.

To practice the double line haul, and generally polish up your casting, take the tip section of a two-piece fly rod and run a line through all the guides except the first one. Strip forty or fifty feet of line out, and put the reel in your pocket. The tip will start to work only after you have twenty to thirty feet of line extended, but being a short, sensitive "rod," it will demand perfect timing. When you can lay out sixty or seventy feet of line this way, you won't have any trouble with a full grown rod. Use a piece of wool to replace the fly when practicing. The narrow, fast line loop will travel close to your ear, and it can be dangerous.

Ellis Newman and I fished the upper Beaverkill this way recently. We used Scotch tape to hold the reel on the tip and improvised a small rod grip by bulking it up. The way I tossed my flies around was a revelation. Tip fishing is good therapy for a man just about the time he thinks he knows something about casting. On the first pool above the dam I sent a half-dozen trout running for cover. After ten minutes of practice the line behaved properly and I managed to catch two small brook trout. They felt like real toughies against nothing but a slim wand of bamboo.

Then a good brown trout jumped out of the water further upstream and I tried to lay a quiet fly over him. This cast landed so hard that the line made a wake from bank to bank. But after an hour or so I had the line shooting out nicely and I landed six trout. Ellis is really quite expert at this sort of thing. In fact, I saw him make a measured cast of 90 feet—without a rod—using an ordinary HCH line. As a hand caster he has no peer.

While the rod is a lever to get the line in motion, neither rod nor line will accomplish anything in particular unless the left hand sets the pace. Although a rod has speed, the speed is latent and must be set in motion to create casting speed. You have to put your car in gear to move forward, or no matter how much you accelerate the engine, the power is wasted. For short casts, little or no line-hand impetus is needed (you don't have to change the speed of a car on a slight curve either), but we are concerned with casts of sixty feet or more—all sharp curves.

There's a tendency these days to get away from the fundamentals of casting and substitute heavyweight gear in its place. Line designers know, for instance, that a heavy torpedo-head line with the weight placed well forward will force a poor caster to increase his speed by virtue of the fact that his rod reaches its deepest resistance to bend with a minimum of line out. This is a legitimate practice. As a matter of fact, it fits in nicely with the poor casting of most anglers. If you don't believe that the average angler is a poor caster, just look at his leader and count the knots in it that aren't part of the taper. However, torpedo-head lines are far from being a cure-all. Do not be misled into thinking that the more weight you pull, the longer the cast.

Weight of a line is important only insofar as it can follow the speed of the man and his rod. Do not assume that a 1-ounce line load will not travel as far as a 1½-ounce line load. Distance depends on *speed*. Speed, in turn, depends on the caster. The analogy here is that there's no reason to believe that a 4,800 pound auto will travel faster than a 2,800 pound auto simply because it is heavier. You might point out that a bait caster can throw a ⅝-ounce weight farther than a ⅜-ounce weight. At first glance it is reasonable, but on second thought you will realize that the problems are those of mechanics—spool, speed, oil density, and friction. Both weights are easily handled by a small child or a grown man. It requires infinitely more effort to set a fly line in motion, and the problems are those of a swordsman—muscular co-ordination, speed, and timing. In distance fly casting, a saturation point exists whereby the caster's muscle limits his efficiency to a certain line weight. The fly caster is pulling and pushing his casting weight—not throwing it off a stick.

Therein lies the fallacy of not considering the importance of the rod in casting. The quality and structure of the rod will determine its vibrational response. A rod is not a bow for an arrow, a spring, a catapult, or a mop handle—it is a moving lever with a moving fulcrum. It is required to transmit the full lever speed magnified by the caster. Its dynamic properties (call it *action*) will in part govern the maximum speed obtainable and the behavior of the line. The system of determining when a rod and line are matched is a hand-and-eye method; the angler must recognize a back cast that moves out smoothly with a minimum of effort, and when fully extended, the weight of the line snuggles ever so slightly against the rod as the stick comes back to a casting bend. This overall relationship is one that writers have been trying to describe for years and has been vaguely referred to as "balance." In no sense is anything balanced. The length of the line extended which creates maximum casting speed is the line load, specified in terms of weight (measured in grains or ounces). Every line has a point of lift (which may be 35, 38, 48, or any number of feet), and this is the weight the maker built into his line in order to pull the shooting line to its maximum distance. We say, for instance, that the lift of a certain tournament line is 62 feet, and it weighs one ounce, but the important load, the frictional load, is heavier. Some people aren't strong enough to pull 1-ounce of line off the water when it's stretched out for 62 feet because the surface resistance against the line is terrific. A line is not lifted up and down, but slid off the water to a supporting cushion of air—endwise to the direction of motion. It stays up there because of its own velocity which you gave it from your hand by means of a rod. Your hands then start the forward propelling motions, and the line goes its merry way; the rod collapses and you stand there holding the cow by the tail. The line was out of rod control at the very instant you started the forward cast. All the gyrations the bamboo goes through (known as harmonics), once the hand has said "forward," are completely without casting significance. The fact that a stick gets the bends after the line loop is formed might be of academic interest to a bridge builder, but is completely useless to an angler.

One morning, many years ago, on Paradise Creek in Pennsylvania, I rounded a sharp bend in the river and saw a large brown trout lying in shallow water just a few yards from shore. The fish obviously didn't see me, as he continued to push his snout against the surface, sucking in an occasional insect. In all my years of angling since that day, I have never bumped into a better setup. Old brown trout don't feed often, and rarely in shallow water under a bright sun. When a big one gets out of his depth he's an easy mark. His black spots looked as thick as a leopard's, and the longer I stood there, the bigger he got. While the trout was still feeding I began to lengthen line, and when everything seemed just right, the cast went out. My trout vanished instantly. The leader had wrapped around the line and the whole mess lay in a heap on the water.

This kind of casting was so common during my first two years of fishing that I imagined getting a straight line out was fifty per cent luck. My source of instruction at the time was a movie-gram booklet, illustrated with a series of casting profiles, and, like most condensed courses, it neglected to look *down* on the angler. This neglect makes a cast one-dimensional—which it is not.

In the good books of fly casting we sometimes read about "casting planes"—those imaginary areas through which the line travels backward and forward. I think this topic is badly undernourished and deserves more food for thought. The loose conception is that the line is flipped back over the caster's head and then shot forward when the rod develops enough resistance to bend. Because of the common belief that a fly rod is a giant spring which responds to the backward momentum of the line, this back flipping and forward shooting is assumed to be working in a single plane. But fly rods are not springs—they add nothing to the speed or distance of a cast as such—and thus, we might ask ourselves if it is necessary to cast like a man cocking a fly swatter and swatting. Or cocking a tack hammer and hammering? The answer is definitely "No."

Straight back and forward casting is difficult to master, and there's some question in my mind whether this "classic" style isn't an impractical standard to set for the beginner. I think it would be much more to the point to take a bird's-eye view of casting and learn something about line behavior. Most casters operate with a slight rotary motion—generally the back cast is tipped off vertical, and the forward cast comes into a true vertical plane. This is achieved by a slight twist of the wrist. When viewed from above, the path of the rod tip would follow a narrow oval—the whole movement being so perfectly blended that it feels, and appears, like a straight back-and-forth motion. Of course the illusion becomes the ideal, particularly to a beginner, and one of the finer points of good fly casting is lost. The symptoms are: knots in the leader, the leader tangling with line, the line tangling with the rod, or any combination of all three. Proper separation of the casting planes is just as important as stance, grip, power application, and other more obvious ingredients of a cast.

Fishing long calm stretches of stream is a trying business. It's both slow and tedious. One bad cast is apt to put down every trout for yards around, and then you have to look for new water. If you wiggle a foot, tell-tale wavelets move out in all directions. When you do make a long, searching cast, every inch has to be fished out before it can be picked up and recast. Now, put a gusty wind over this kind of water—a wind that blows all day long—add a few smart brown trout, and you have a fair picture of the fishing conditions in Belgium. Skilled anglers, however, work with twelve and fifteen feet of fine leader in this cockeyed wind, using light forward-taper lines, and they knock off trout at distances up to seventy and even eighty feet. Until Albert Godart set the pace in the early thirties, the art of dry-fly fishing was a clumsy business in these waters; classical casting style has literally gone with the wind.

Among the skilled fly casters I have watched, Albert Godart is outstanding, in that his own peculiar style of casting has been adopted by a nation of anglers. Godart is not a big man, but he has strong hands and a perfect sense of timing. Whether he's standing on a platform three feet over the water or under the willows in leaky waders, his casting is effortless. In order to keep his international distance title year after year, he had to compete with bigger men and bigger rods; and while Godart got no bigger, his casts always reached out those extra yards for a win.

People who attend tournaments generally lose interest after the first half of the first day, and wander off to visit their friends or take their ease while scores are racked up and time passes. Whenever Godart got on the platform a huge crowd would collect—not just to see the maestro at work, but to try and figure out what he did. He never looked as though he knew what he was doing, particularly when making a backcast. The line traveled so low going backwards that it appeared to be out of control—then it climbed upward as his cast went forward, drifting high overhead for fifty yards. People not only watched, but began imitating, because it seemed like a good fishing cast. It was. On the wide open, wind-blown streams of Belgium, where Godart had fished all his life, he had created a style for distance and delicacy that has a definite role in angling.

In the Belgian style of casting, the wrist twist is exaggerated so that the rod tip (when viewed from above) executes a wide oval in an almost semi-circular path. The line will drop gradually during the first part of the back pull, causing the loop to form horizontally to the ground instead of vertically, but the last few feet of line will rise as the rod tip sweeps forward and upward in the final delivery. This is opposite to a normal back cast which has a tendency to drop instead of rise at full extension. The law of gravity can be almost ignored in any fly cast, as the time factor is so short and the weights concerned so light and bulky, that gravity plays a minor role. Air resistance is almost the only resistance that the caster has to overcome. The result in Godart's case is a high, fast, forward cast, which loses all momentum before dropping to the water, putting the fly down as gently as a natural insect.

The double line haul plays an important role in controlling the speed and direction of the Belgian cast. We know that the left hand should keep the line taut at all times. We know, too, that the left hand can add an extra "pull" to the line and thus create greater speed. On a long cast, the line has a tendency to lose speed and drop to the water behind you, and a slight pull of the left hand just before you start the forward cast will lift the line up. The fact that you can gain control by increasing the speed of the line is important in a cast such as this, where the rod is traveling in two widely separated planes. Use of the double haul is limited in average fishing casts, but a gentle tug is needed to make the line hop up when the Belgian cast is straightening out. If you should attempt this style I'd suggest that you watch the backcast as well as the forward delivery until you get a clear picture of what the line is doing and how your power application is affecting it. But Godart's style is not one that you'll easily copy—the significant and important factor is the line loop and its applications to practical fishing.

The formation of the line loop is one of the most distinctive features of the Belgian style of casting, in that it is horizontal to

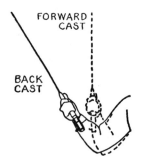

Figure 13. In the Belgian cast, the rod is brought back off-vertical, coming forward in a vertical plane. The whole movement is a smooth, continuous, rotary motion of the arm.

the ground or water, rather than rolling back vertically. By the time it has straightened out, the rod is coming forward in a vertical position and the outgoing loop forms the normal vertical roll. Any line loop, whether vertical or horizontal, can be widened or narrowed by the caster. To narrow the loop down,

Figure 14. With a strong wind blowing from the right, simply reverse the usual casting planes, coming back in the overhead vertical plane and coming forward with the rod tipped off-vertical. This cast won't foul up in the wind, even with a long leader.

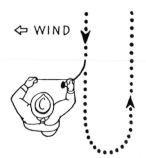

put more emphasis in the tip; to widen the loop, relax your grip, putting less emphasis in the tip and using more arm motion. In the Belgian cast, however, we are more concerned with the function of the loop than we are with its appearance.

Properly executed, this is a wide-looped cast, and the wider and faster it's made, and the slower the loop unfolds, the greater the distance achieved. There's a physical limit to how wide and how fast you can work, the whole procedure depending on "pinch" and wrist power. Albert Godart's hand would give you an idea of the demands made physically. His casting thumb is

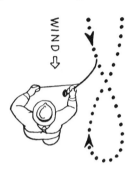

Figure 15. In the face of strong winds a narrow figure eight cast will keep your casting planes well separated. If the wind comes from the rear, simply reverse the cast, as though the arrows in the diagram were pointing in the opposite direction.

twice as broad as the one on his left hand. This is because of the terrific squeeze he puts into his casts when handling a long line. For purposes of fishing, however, the Belgian style requires no more effort than an up-and-down stroke.

There are variations of this cast for different wind conditions.

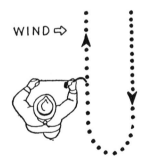

Figure 16. With a strong wind coming from the left, the regular Belgian cast will not foul the line or leader. This is a bird's eye view of the cast shown in Figure 13.

To work with a strong wind blowing from the right, for instance, the cast is reversed; the rod comes back vertically, and goes forward off vertical, forming the horizontal loop in reverse order. The so-called figure-eight cast is also a variant of the Belgian style, a narrow eight being used in the face of strong winds (see Figure 15) and a wider eight being used with gusty or back winds. With the wind blowing from the left, the regular Belgian cast will lay out a long line (see Figure 16). All of these casts keep the leader from tangling with the line because the casting planes are completely separated.

To get at the core of the Belgian style of casting, consider the physical behavior of the line. In a perfectly outstretched back cast of any kind, every inch of line has identical velocity—only the momentum varies, and this in direct proportion to the belly weight. When the rod comes forward, momentum and velocity decline very quickly; the momentum of the front taper drops more rapidly than that of the heavier belly section. The weight and inertia of the shooting line also demand work of the belly section, in being pulled forward. Thus, the burden of maintaining velocity of the taper falls on the belly—which is pushing, pulling, and carrying its own weight. If the amount of energy given the cast is just barely enough to straighten the belly, then the forward taper will never straighten, but flop alongside the belly. This is a common malady when casting against strong winds—the heavier belly section maintains its velocity out of proportion to the front taper which declines at an ever greater rate than normal.

The conclusion from my experience is—the longer you can delay complete unrolling of the forward loop, the longer the cast will be, provided the belly of the line maintains its velocity. Line taper plays an important role in delaying the loop, particularly the back taper of a weight-forward line, which acts like the tail on a kite. The kite would be the belly section. Casting in a single up-and-down, or back-and-forth plane minimizes this possibility. I believe the instant formation of a line loop that pulls shooting line at a maximum is not as effective as it has been heretofore thought. A more delayed pull can give a more gradual and prolonged flight to the line. Straight back-and-forth casting will not accomplish this. The distance cast as executed by people who really have to reach out is more of a half-side-swipe aimed the way you'd lob out a mortar shell—way up—the belly section coming to pull only when the long back taper is exhausting its momentum.

To delay the loop, you need a wide loop to start with, and this only comes through complete separation of the casting planes. With the line unrolling in its forward flight, the part that has unrolled is the only part that is pulling more line out. Obviously, it's easier to pull shooting line than a heavy belly section that has already gone around the loop. If the loop is narrow you are wasting energy to unfold the cast, whereas the initial momentum should be given to a wide loop that will straighten by its dying gasps.

Free-form casting has become much more popular in the U. S., and I must admit after more than twenty years of fishing on windy bonefish and tarpon flats where it may gust to 20 or 25 knots and any cast *under* 60 feet won't even reach a fish—the Godart style of casting makes sense. As I said in Chapter II, a high back cast is fundamental and must be learned by the beginner until he acquires the speed and control to shoot from all angles. One of the characteristics of a graphite rod is its high resistance to bending, which increases the speed of recovery; I believe this will prove to be a great advantage for the average hand in achieving distance. With a strong wind blowing from behind you can literally punch a back cast low in the rear (a high back cast in this case quickly loses velocity as a greater length is exposed to the wind), and recover fast enough to shoot a long forward cast. Even the very light graphite trout rods that I have been using this past season have proven their worth under the worst wind conditions.

Albert Godart made his last cast some years ago, as did Ellis Newman, Johnny Dieckman, Jon Tarantino, and Pierre Creusevaut, all of whom were great anglers; I fished with each of them. They had absolutely nothing in common as far as casting is concerned, except for being champions. No matter how often the double haul is described you will always find it somewhat different as each caster develops his individual style.

CHAPTER X

Bucktails and Streamer Flies

DISCOVERY PASSAGE, the twisting gut that cuts Vancouver Island from the mainland of British Columbia, shimmered under the hot September sun. The tide was slack in this one motionless hour before north-run water turns south, and the long rubbery arms of kelp sprawled torpidly from their rock-rooted bases. From trap-rock ledges crowning the islands which dot the Passage—granite islands that stretch and dip as if feeling for the bottom—sharp-eyed gulls examined the face of the quiet water. Two miles away, the spiny coastal range of the mainland towered amid the silent march of clouds.

Then languorously the ponderous tentacles of kelp began to stretch. A sluggish creeping, a wakening quiver, a spasmodic straightening and then a sudden swift arching to the south exposed millions of small emerald-backed fish whose lives depended on the sanctuary of those leafy arms. Longer and darker forms rising from far below grouped in vicious waves which surged to the surface and bolted through the defenseless fry. The air was rent by the screaming of hovering gulls. Slate-and-white bodies plummeted in wild dives to meet the rise and fall of the silvery needlefish. The tide had turned, whirling and eddying in the magic of a second. I guided a tuft of glistening bear hair through the desperate flurries of cohoe salmon. It was the perfect setting for streamer fly-fishing.

Three thousand miles to the east, in a lake that sprawls in down timber, pale green smelt schooled at a stream mouth, moving cautiously along the white sand floor. Sticklebacks and mottled darters pushed against the whispering current, seeking the icy water that bubbled from the sand. Great green shadows crouching behind rock, spectral creatures flattening their bellies against gravel, watched in the silence of a transparent world. Slowly the trap closed. Longer and grayer forms moved over the shelf into shoal water. The big-eyed smelt sucked at frail waltzing midges, spent mayflies and creepers drifting in the current, and minute plankton exploding from weed beds. The first chill wind of evening whirled across the surface as the trout moved in. I tugged a delicate gray feathered streamer through widening rings. This too was a perfect setting for streamer fly fishing—even though Maine and the Passage are a continent apart.

From Cape Mudge to Munsungun, in all the rivers and bayous between; from the thunderous roll of the cohoe in saltchuck to the soundless drift of togue in the thoroughfare . . . the tempo changes from West to East, from cypress swamp to frigid Arctic water, but the theme is the same. When fat, sea-run cutthroat rise at the last of the ebb tide, and the bright steelhead, hatchet-faced and hard, cruise into holding water, an angler with the fly reaps his reward. He may possess the most perfect rod with line to match, waders, brogues and clothing beyond the layman's comprehension, but his gains depend on one small object—a feathered confidence dancing to the rhythm of the rod.

A fly reflects the character of the water in which it is used, the character of the fish for which it was designed, and the convictions of its creator. The staid simplicity of a chalk-stream dun, somber, fragile, and small; the wild spirit of a steelhead fly, gaudy and coarse, lusty as a coastal river. Yet each is dressed in a conventional shape—hairs, feathers, tinsels—the ingredients being a result of experience or experiment. Once conceived, they become patterns. Favored with success, properly aged, written of, spoken of and commercialized, they become standard patterns.

The streamer fly of conventional shape is long and minnow-like, true to its purpose. Wherever big fish eat little fish—and this is a universal predilection—the slim feathered lure will take its toll. To endow it with the wavering flight of a minnow, the angler must be a master impressionist, a rod-tip sorcerer who can infuse life and breath into the sunken fly. The streamer is a flexible lure; it can be cast upstream, down, cross-stream, and back. Its field of play is limitless, but without a touch of leger-demain it resembles nothing but feathers.

The streamer fly consists basically of long hackle feathers tied parallel to the hook shank, extending to or slightly beyond the hook bend. In some cases hackle feather and hair are combined in one wing, or else they are tied to give depth to the body, with hackle-feather wing above the hook and polar-bear hair below. Closely allied to this type of lure is the bucktail. The word "bucktail" was originally intended to cover minnow-like flies with wings made from the tail of a buck deer. Shortly thereafter flies were made of polar, black and brown bear hair, moose mane, skunk hair, and whatnot. Few fishermen could distinguish deer from bear hair, so in the resulting confusion of minnow-like flies with hair wings, they were dubbed "bucktails." The effective-ness of either type of fly is governed by the length, color, and inherent action.

For a good many years early in my fishing career I fished with bucktails and streamer flies almost exclusively. They are easy to tie, and, in the eyes of a youngster, easy to associate with catch-ing fish. In that water on the East Branch of the Delaware from Shinhopple down the main branch to Port Jervis were some of the greatest bass pools in the country. There still are. But the smallmouths are not as easy to catch as they were then. It didn't take long to find that simple brown-and-white and black-and-white bucktails which represented the many brook minnows and shiners were more effective than the fancy dressings which Dan Todd copied from the catalogues of New England tackle houses.

Our fishing was distinctly and totally different. We used the standard thin silver or gold tinsel body with these wings for trout bucktails, and the fat full-bodied red, yellow, or black wool bodies ribbed with tinsel for bass. Delaware smallmouths like a fuller shape and a bit more color in their bucktails. To make closer imitations of certain minnows we used hackle feather wings, and these streamers had a definite role in late summer, low-water fishing. The barred killifish was represented in patterns tied with a barred-rock hackle feather. The pronounced dark vertical stripes simulate closely the markings of this species. A pattern such as the Grizzly Gray streamer is close to the ones we made. Then there were the bridled minnows, a group of minnows collectively called "pin minnows" in Vermont and New Hampshire, as we later learned; these have a dark, in many cases pronounced, stripe running down the lateral line. Here the badger-hackle feather wing is the minnow's counterpart, particularly that feather known as "golden" badger. Most of the laterally marked minnows are straw-colored overall, with a silvery belly. The Northern sculpin turned up in bass and trout stomachs so often that Dan and I worked hard on getting a useful imitation, and these patterns revolved around strips of hen pheasant wing laid over bucktail to create that mottled brown form. Eventually we decided that the only important thing about the sculpin was the way he swam—in short hops and darts along the bottom. This discovery busted Hale's Eddy wide open one morning when we caught about twenty bass and trout by fishing the fly in that manner.

Some white or yellow is essential in all bucktails that I use. These are the backgrounds for any other color. In fact an all white or all yellow bucktail with tinsel body often is good, and in my experience this is not true of black or red except when they are tied with marabou wings. But first in importance is black combined with white, then brown and white, and then white combined with bright red. In waters where dace are abundant, I like brown combined with yellow using a gold tinsel body. Black and yellow, or black combined with orange are effective sometimes, but in the streams I fish regularly these two wings are not nearly as good as the others. Blue and green are poor takers unless combined with white in a regular hackle feather wing, and even then I've found such dressings sporadic in their results on our Delaware watershed. Yet the blues and greens are of first importance further east, especially in Maine.

Maine has given bountifully to the lore of the streamer fly. The Ghost family, the famed Gray and Black originated by Carrie Stevens of Upper Dam; the Green, Lady, and Silver Ghosts; and, still awaiting its acceptance through trial and story, the colorful Galloping Ghost—all are products of the late Bert Quimby. Bert is responsible also for six bucktail patterns known as the Trout Rock series; in addition, the Hurricane, Chief Needahbeh, Nimrod, Ross McKenny—in all, he has some thirty patterns to his credit, and the majority are already standard. Bill Edson's Tigers—the Light and Dark—born on the waters of Dennysville, are known from coast to coast. More recently, the Nine-three, Green King, and Barnes Special came tumbling out of the cold lakes country, products of the forties. But their sphere of influence becomes spotty as the angler heads west. The feather wing streamer is less popular in the Pacific area where the minnow fly is used chiefly for steelhead and silver salmon. A hair wing is much more durable between the jaws of either one. Much of this fishing is done in salt and brackish water where large forage fish are common, and the hair wing is more easily tied and more readily cast in four- and five-inch lengths. As a result, the tall tree country leans to patterns like the Candlefish, Skykomish Sunrise, Coronation, the late Jim Pray's Owl-Eyed Optic and Thor Bucktail, the Umpqua Special, and Fred Reed's Orange Steelheader. There are feather wing streamers peculiar to the West like the Chappie by C. L. Franklin, and the Spruce by Roy Donnelly, but by and large the trend is to hair wings—bucktail and polar bear hair. Each new watershed develops its own patterns, which is as it should be.

My first fly rod was a very long one, a seamed tubular steel affair not unlike a series of umbrella staves jointed together. I don't remember how long it was, but I did have good control over my line because of the length, a factor that is usually missing in my streamer work today. Now that I own a closet full of rods, I never seem to have the right one with me when the time comes to play a minnow fly through difficult places. The ideal rod for fishing streamer flies would be about 9½-feet in length, but such a rod, being adapted to nothing but streamer flies, has a practical disadvantage. The closest I have been able to come to the long rod, still maintaining maximum capacity in its other functions with the dry and wet fly, is an 8-foot, 8½-inch medium action. This length has good control over the streamer when working across varying currents. By holding the tip high, most of the belly portion of the line can be eliminated from the surface, thereby reducing drag and permitting a hand to fly sensitivity that would be lost with a heavy submerged line. A rod takes a beating when you're casting a fly as heavy as a bucktail and lifting it out of the water as is frequently necessary. This is one reason why I always suggest an 8½-foot, or even 9-foot rod for the novice. While my tubular steel rod was only a sad imitation of what a good fly rod should be, the way it handled a bucktail was a pure delight.

Under normal stream conditions, the minnow-type fly is cast across and downstream, allowing the lure to drift with the current. An occasional movement of the rod keeps the bucktail alive, and when all the slack is out of the line, the fly is retrieved back upstream in short pulls. The darting motion of the bucktail should be very short and spaced at regular intervals to simulate a small minnow struggling against the current. Before the cast is fully retrieved, it often pays to let the fly drift back downstream

as though dead, and then repeating the swim. Remember to keep
your rod parallel to the surface, and retrieve by stripping the
line over your rod-hand finger. Many good fish are missed by
anglers who retrieve by swinging the rod around to a position
where they can't strike when the fish hits.

In my opinion, the successful use of the streamer and bucktail
fly has been limited to a few experienced fishermen because they
change their strategy with their lures. Random casting with these
flies is disappointing because the fish that will take them are not
nearly as plentiful as those that will take dry and wet flies. You
must first learn to recognize favorable situations. One place,
for instance, is in the feeding runs above big still holes where
large trout may lie undisturbed during the day. About a half-
hour after the sun leaves the water, these trout are active. If a
bucktail or streamer is allowed to work in the current, darted
here and there but seldom withdrawn, it often gets results. In the
middle of the day, if the fly is sunk deep and idled around,
allowed to eddy and move in the bottom currents, and seldom
retrieved, a big trout can be tantalized. This is the secret of
streamer fly-fishing. It makes trout suspicious to withdraw the
fly suddenly and often. About the time a fish makes up his mind
to take it—and they don't hurry in making up their minds—the
fly is pulled out of the water.

One of the most expert streamer fly makers and streamer fly
fishermen of my acquaintance is Lew Oatman of Shusman, New
York. Lew has put a great deal of time and thought into this
branch of angling, and I think a letter he wrote to me last summer concerning a trip on the Battenkill River will give you a
clear idea of how a specialist evaluates the proper conditions for
using a minnow-type fly:

> There were a number of small trout in the pools but the larger
> fish seemed to be in the riffles, especially where a big pool spilled
> over at the tail, and in the hiding places under roots and cut banks
> where the current was moving. I saw only one big trout in a pool

and he lay in a crevice of a rock ledge in the Buffum's Bridge Pool and looked to be about twenty inches long. I couldn't start him. Several other anglers tried for him but I think after watching him that he was feeding on crawfish. I caught one trout about a foot long and two or three smaller ones on wet flies and nymphs and after realizing that the big trout were in fast water I decided to use streamer flies.

I have been wanting to fish the Vermont side, so I went to Arlington, bought my license and started right at the edge of the village below the dam. When I waded out into the riffles below the dam pool I saw a pocket about twenty feet in diameter right in the middle of the riffle. I worked my streamer across stream just above the pocket on the first cast, and on the next cast about three feet lower when this big trout struck. He proved to be 19¼-inches long. He was all over the riffle and out of the water two or three times before I could net him. It's funny, but I don't remember large brown trout jumping out of the water except for those I've taken in the past three or four years. Since then nearly every good brown I have caught has come clear out of the water. Have you noticed that? I mentioned that to Mr. Prindle who fishes the Kill steadily and he agreed.

Below there the stream didn't look like big trout water and I changed to a wet light cahill and caught three brook trout from 8 to 10 inches and by that time was down where I met my mother and sister for a picnic lunch on the wood road between Arlington to the Sandgate church. That is a beautiful spot with the river right beside the road and the bank above covered with maiden hair ferns.

After lunch I went down to where the Roaring Branch flows into the Kill. There are good hiding places under the banks and trees and pockets where the currents come together, and I hooked a sixteen inch brown in there on a streamer. I figured that one would just about make my limit of five pounds so I went down to the Tackle Box to brag a little. Mrs. Brown took a picture of them. The big trout was the largest brought in there so far this year.

I caught these two on flies practically identical to two I tie regularly, but I tied these two the night before I started and when I tie for myself I always seem to experiment and come up with something a little different. The 19-inch trout took a streamer like the silver Darter except that I had tied one clear blue feather in between the badger wings and made the body solid silver. The 16-inch trout took a fly like the Golden Darter except that I had tied a small bunch of brown bucktail in under the wings and cocked them a little higher. I believe that either of these trout would have taken either fly or either of the standard patterns I tie or for that matter, any good imitation of a shiner or black nosed dace because most of the minnows I saw were one or the other. Although it is possible that the all silver body shows up better in the rough water I was fishing, but the standard body would be preferable in clear or quieter water. Perhaps I should tie both so a fisherman could change according to the type of water he was in, and still have a good shiner or a good black nosed dace.

The more I fish for, and observe big trout the more convinced I am that they spend most of their time in out of the way places and fishermen are likely to walk past such places and spend their time fishing the big beautiful pools. And also if a man will get good imitations of two or three common minnows and then fish thoroughly and patiently he will catch his share of the good ones. It has also been my experience that I have caught most of my big trout between noon and two o'clock. It is true that most of the hatches occur in the evening but big trout seldom feed on them except where big flies like the drakes are hatching and there are enough smaller trout thrashing around after them to excite big ones in that same pool. I don't ever remember a big trout having a pool more or less to himself, ever rising to a hatch of flies.

The technique for bass is not quite the same. In general, we look for bass in the same places we look for big trout. That the two species use the same shelter is not unusual. On the Delaware River for instance, many of the largest trout are taken after several bass have been removed from the very same hole. But the bass fisherman using bucktails has more water to play with because the bronzeback wanders around much more than trout do, and frequently in broad daylight they will chase minnows up into water so shallow that their dorsals show above the surface. On most bass rivers, the fish generally hold toward the head of the eddies where they can watch the moving water for food. A bucktail cast across the current and retrieved in a skittering manner will arouse these bass; often a smallmouth will follow the bucktail all the way across the river, taking it just when your retrieve stops.

One of the most common mistakes made by beginners when using the streamer fly is to drop the lure on top of the fish. This direct approach is not the manner in which a minnow would come to a trout. The fly should come to the holding water with the current, the line being held carefully cross-stream from the trout's position. The best procedure is to cast the streamer slightly up and across stream, causing the submerged fly to swing down in a curve. By jerking the rod tip as the fly follows the natural path of the line, and stripping in short lengths to exaggerate the action, the fly eventually reaches a point directly downstream and is then worked back, whereupon the line is shortened and picked up for the next cast. This is a comfortable, if not always productive, way to fish.

I have experienced remarkable fishing in big, fast rivers by letting a streamer fly drift with the current on a long slack line, getting it down into white water directly below me, then retrieving with the rod held high above my head and making the fly bounce from one rip to the next. This is a particularly good method in shallow, broken areas where there is no evidence of holding water. Lightly dressed streamers such as the Black Ghost are ideal for this type of fishing. Many times I've had big salmon pop out of what looked like barren water, leaping clear of the surface and snatching at the fly on the way down.

In lake fishing, the streamer fly is most difficult to use properly. Here there is no helpful current to animate the feathers. Most anglers try to reach out as far as possible, and then, by stripping the line in even pulls, bring the lure back minnow-fashion. That is easy. But for the most part it is not wholly effective. The fly should sink deep and be retrieved erratically, fast and slow, in long and short pulls, as well as being worked at the surface in mechanical jerks. The expert streamer fisherman will bring the fly back in various depths and speeds with each cast.

In a great many cases the trolled streamer fly is more effective than one that is cast. This is particularly true of early-season landlocked salmon fishing, when the angler must buck strong winds. Although this is contrary to popular practise there is a good reason for it. Admittedly the trolled fly is a steadily moving form, one that in a short area may simulate the flight of a smelt. But the important point is that the fly is moving constantly and without hesitation for a long distance (something which you could not accomplish when casting), and landlocks often follow a fly for long distances before finally making up their minds. Trolling keeps the angler moving away from his quarry, the far-off disturbance of the canoe having little significance; whereas a follow-up to the side of a stationary canoe exposes the angler and his rod. To further establish the indifference salmon and squaretails have toward boat noises, it is a common practice to troll in the wake of an outboard, catching fish on the trolled streamer a few yards astern. There are streamer flies tied especially for trolling, incidentally, but they are used almost exclusively in Maine and the Pacific Northwest. The trolling streamer gets a big play among landlocked salmon and silver salmon anglers. It consists of two hooks tied in tandem (these are joined by means of nylon, wire, or bead chain), and this construction serves a dual purpose; it permits tying a long slim fly which simulates more closely the smelt, candlefish, and herring where a single hook would be completely overdressed, and the extra hook gets any short-striking fish. Such flies cannot be cast successfully because the wing gets fouled up with the hooks. But under the conditions they are designed for, trolling streamers are better than regular-length streamer flies.

I think the most telling addition to my streamer fly work has been the use of marabou flies. We never got around to using them until just before I left the Delaware country, and I think if Dan Todd knew about them earlier, we would have taken most of those cannibals we had to get with live bait. We were fishing one of the big pools above Harvard one morning, when Dan spotted a nice smallmouth in a pocket where the stream splits. The fish held against an undercut bank behind a pile of brush. It was Dan's claim, so I sat on a stump and watched. He made three bad casts, but the bass didn't see them. The fourth cast clunked the water hard right over the fish, but no sooner had the bass ducked for cover than the marabou began working and the smallmouth wheeled right out again. The old bass followed the fly for a few feet, then slipped back toward the bank. The next few casts were good ones, with the streamer drifting back to the fish, and each time the smallmouth followed the marabou back upstream, getting more and more excited. Finally, he put one more cast in that pocket and retrieved it very slowly, and when the marabou reached the brush where Dan couldn't get any more line the bass said, "The devil with this" and ripped into the fly. That started Dan on marabous. I had to wait until the following spring on the Esopus before I was completely sold.

I missed the early run of rainbows that year. There were a thaw and a flood in February, and by the time trout season opened in April most of the big rainbows had been up and back. The water was lower than usual, and clear, too clear for big trout, I thought, but I went down to the Seven Arch riff just the same. This is spotty fishing at best, and the most I dared hope for was an occasional spent fish heading back to the reservoir.

A pair of smolts, their parr markings carelessly hidden under loose silver scales, fell to the first two casts. Both of these little fellows came from behind a large boulder that rested close to my side of the stream, so I put the Light Tiger streamer in my keeper ring and went up on the bank to rest the water for awhile. I had a good view of the eddy from where I sat and by watching very closely soon made out the forms of at least a dozen small rainbows darting back and forth. Then, well to the rear, perhaps twenty-five feet below the boulder, I saw what could have been a slab of rock, a sucker, a walleyed pike—or what I was looking for.

Getting the streamer down to this fish without getting hung in the ambush of smolts meant a long cross-stream cast, beyond the eddy, and a short drift followed by working the fly on the swing so that it would come to the lair below the little ones and over the big one. In short, it meant holding a slack belly in the line on several speeds of current. The problem of the cast was more interesting than the fishing.

On the first swing around, the trout flashed behind the streamer and settled back to the bottom. The second, and then the third accomplished nothing at all. I cut the Light Tiger off and tied on a No. 8 Black Marabou. I remembered doing this once before to amuse a fat smallmouth on the Cacapon River in West Virginia; he had been so amused that he ended up in a frying pan—and this was the precedent I had to go by. Rarely does the angler find a more satisfactory reason for choosing flies, particularly streamers.

The marabou followed the same path as its predecessor, and just as it reached a point opposite the trout, I raised the rod tip and began a painfully slow, twitching retrieve. The black stork feathers quivered and fluttered, opening and closing like the fingers of a hypnotist. I was prepared for the strike as the big rainbow came to the fly with the paced certainty of a dentist pulling a tooth.

Pulling across current, the fish bored immediately for the far side of the river. The frail bamboo quivered with every move. Changing tactics, the trout raced into the current below me and stopped in midstream to tug frantically at the straining rod. Giving all the line I dared, I backed out of deep water, reached the bank, and trotted through the shallows to get below him. The rainbow sensed this shift of pressure and continued downstream into faster water, which still left me in the rear. I splashed along, retrieving line and trying to bring him into the shallows. Not once did the fish jump, which made my work all the harder. It wasn't until we had covered several hundred yards of stream that he made his mistake by turning to fight the current. I weighed him at the lunch wagon in Phoenicia that afternoon—a 6-pound male, with deep pink-purple sash and a knoblike kype on his lower jaw.

This happened many years ago, and needless to say, I've been a marabou addict ever since. Although my collection of marabous has expanded in recent years, the small black one still heads the list for Eastern trout fishing. White has proved to be the best for Western waters and for landlocked salmon fishing, and yellow or orange for bass. I think the orange would go well for salmon and steelheads. However, I have never tried it for these species. The marabou must be properly tied. If the tier uses the wrong part of the plume or too much of it when making the wing, the fly will be absolutely worthless. Many marabous simply mat together in the water—these serve no purpose at all. A good one, one that pulses and flutters at the slightest pressure, will excite any kind of gamefish; if the wing doesn't work, the fly won't produce. The topping of a marabou generally consists of peacock herl or dyed ostrich herl. For the black pattern I have never found need of any topping, but for the others it undoubtedly adds to their effectiveness. The best procedure to follow in making a marabou is to use two matched plumes, one-third longer than the hook and placed so that the feathers curve out. A modified sproat bend, 3X and 4X long in No. 6 to No. 10 for general purposes, and No. 2 to No. 6 for steelheads and salmon would be just about right.

Polly Rosborough, the originator of the Silver Garland Marabou, a pattern that has struck great popularity in the West, tops his flies with four colors of ostrich herl, starting with a very pale, yellowish olive, next, medium olive, dark olive, and then finishes with three or four strands of black—a blending that gives the illusion of a small chub in the water. Bass fishermen in Arizona are partial to brown topping, while on the other side of the lake in Nevada they want deep blue. Yes, there's dissension in Lake Meade. I wouldn't be too concerned with collecting marabou versions of standard patterns, such as a Royal Coachman Marabou, Black Ghost Marabou, or what have you—this is clearly gilding the lily. The quality of the feather and the general color scheme are the deciding factors. Both the Royal and the Ghost have white wings, and it is more practical to select marabous of different wing colors or with various toppings, before you end up with too many flies that look alike. In the case of the Silver Garland Marabou, I imagine the body plays an important role. Polly uses silver garland (Christmas decoration) of about lead-pencil thickness for body material which gives flash and form to the moving fly. I like this body so well that I'm adding it to all my marabous. If a river is broad, turbulent, or off-color, the chances of a showy fly, say a white or yellow marabou, in attracting fish seem greater than the gray or black wing.

Some fisheries men working in the state of Illinois back in 1939 recorded the fact that fishing improved as the water transparency increased (Bennett, Thompson and Parr). This bit of research was done on Fork Lake, Illinois, and refers to largemouth bass and bluegills. A careful record was kept of the man hours of fishing, the catch, and the water transparency at the time. It was found that when the transparency ranged from ½ to 2 feet, the number of fish caught per man hour was 2.04; from 2 to 2½ feet the catch was 2.86; from 3½ to 4½ feet it was 6.53 fish per man hour. The reason given for better fishing during clear water periods was the fact that the bass and bluegills hunted their food by sight—which is true of many species to a greater

or lesser extent. Be that as it may, it's easy to see that in discolored water the showy lure has an advantage.

Many anglers use it as a locator-fly in clear water by teasing
it in and out of eddies, behind boulders, and working it over hold
after hold. Invariably a fish will come to it, sometimes taking it,
but at the very least, visibly excited by the motion of the wings.
The procedure then is to change to a small wet fly and work the
holding water after a few minutes' rest, or continue downstream
after marking the location, saving the fish for a tactic that takes
shape later in the day. It is a profitable method of fishing a
strange river. I don't claim to be the originator of the tandem
marabou and wet-fly rig, but it occurred to me a number of
years ago that with a small wet fly tied in from the bend of the
marabou hook, some of the located fish might very well take the
fly—if not the attractor. I was fishing the water below Hunter,
on the Schoharie River, that day, and after raising a number of
trout who wanted to play only with the marabou, I clinched on
a six-inch strand of nylon and a small hackle pattern. It was
an offensive looking thing, but before long a trout slipped up
behind the white ostrich plumes, and after a few tentative nips
at the marabou, he snapped around and swallowed the little wet
fly. This is a typical strike, and is apparently earned through the
provocative action of the streamer.

Interestingly enough there is a similar cast using a bucktail
and wet-fly combination. The bucktail is tied in as a tail fly,
and a small wet pattern is tied up the leader as a dropper fly.
It is generally understood that this represents a minnow chasing
an insect when the cast is drawn through the water. However,
the fish don't always follow the logical sequence of grabbing the
bucktail and then the wet fly. Often as not, they dash ahead of
the "minnow" and take the insect. This two-fly cast supplies the
need for a showy fly to get the fish's attention; however, it offers
a smaller fly to arouse the appetite. Frankly, I haven't found it

too productive on trout, but for bluegills and bass this bucktail attractor is often useful.

There doesn't seem to be any tangible connection between marabous and "fished-out" waters, but I've often found this streamer most deadly in rivers that have been hammered to what appears to be depletion. There's a long stretch of flat water on the East Branch of the Delaware, for instance, that flows away from the road below Arena. If you stumbled on it in late summer, you wouldn't notice the old packages of fish hooks, lunch boxes, tin cans, odd shoes and flotsam that were left at various levels of the river—starting high in the alders in early spring and stretching over exposed gravel to the lowest ebb. It's like following the tide marks of the ocean. The lush countryside quickly hides the footprints of men who combed the water mercilessly in the first two months. But in late summer, the river is left to itself. Looking at the flat from the suspension bridge was enough to discourage anybody. It was late August and the river was so low that it was barely moist. A clear, amber glow sparkled over the polished rocks of the stream bed. Not a rising fish, not even a chub disturbed the mirrored surface. Somewhere below I knew a trout must be. They always are.

I walked a long distance downriver that August morning and fished back up with a No. 10 marabou. Once I changed to a No. 8 white marabou and caught a rainbow that hefted close to four pounds. But the white marabou was lost in a heavy brown trout that came from under a stump in the very next pool. The fish turned, wrapping the leader around some roots, and it broke off before I could get to him. Changing back to the black fly I proceeded to take six trout which averaged about one pound in weight and another rainbow that was almost as big as the first. I had seen this water fished day after day in the summer without so much as a fingerling coming to an angler's fly. None of the trout I caught that day were feeding fish—they seemed to come from under or behind rock jumbles and stumps, spots that I had covered a thousand times before with wet and dry flies. Suffice to say, when an educated trout finally meets a marabou, anything can happen.

There's only one technique to acquire when marabou fishing. Learn to fish it slowly, with all the twitching and motion you can put into the feathers. Last fall on the Ash River in British Columbia, I covered the tail of a pool thoroughly, not once, but three times. On the third time around I made a long cast to what looked like holding water and mended my line to get all the slack I could in order to prolong the drift. By bouncing my rod tip up and down, the movement set up enough motion in the streamer to keep it fluttering as it drifted slowly with the current. The next thing I knew I was looking at the belly of a high-flying steelhead. The slow active drift is a positively deadly approach when regular retrieves are useless.

I don't believe there's any species of fish that won't take a marabou. Its victims range from chinook salmon (the Silver Garland nailed a 52-pounder in salt water) all the way down to panfish. In salt water I've used marabous to good effect on striped bass, weakfish, snook, bluefish and ladyfish. Last summer I made a day's trip to a nearby New York river, one that has a rather democratic fish population, and caught rock bass, brook, brown, and rainbow trout, largemouth and smallmouth bass, pickerel, and perch—and all on the same fly. Very few fly types can inspire such a variety of fish. The marabou certainly isn't infallible, but if you're stepping into a river with a mixed fish population it has greater general appeal than nymphs or wet and dry flies. It is so completely different that I believe the fish are confused by it; big bass and trout often swim around and around the marabou, their fins fanning overtime before abruptly slamming into the feathers. It is well to remember this characteristic strike and always give the fly plenty of time in the water —even when no follow-up is apparent.

While fishing on the North Branch of the Au Sable in Michi-

gan late one spring, I found a large brown trout hanging around
a log jam. The stream bottom is mostly sand and silt with a fine
cover of gravel, so it was an easy task to wade into position
without disturbing this fish. I've often wondered since, just what
the trout was doing. He just whirled around in small circles
looking very much as if he were chasing his tail. This was a well-
conditioned brown, thick of body and strong of muscle. For a
moment I was so confused by its gyrations that I did nothing but
stand and look. Fortunately his size subdued my curiosity and
there began one of the most exasperating half-hours ever spent.

The trout didn't even see the first five or six casts—he was still
busy chasing himself. I nearly broke out laughing when he
stopped long enough to look at the marabou. He studied it for
a moment and then cruised along behind. I had only about thirty
feet of water between his position and mine to get him interested enough to swallow the fly. When the fish was a few feet
away from me he turned and went back from whence he came.
This was repeated about a half-dozen times, and on each trip the
big trout was getting less excited about his tail and more excited
about the marabou. Oddly enough, my presence didn't seem to
matter. I worked slowly and deliberately with no sudden motions that might put him down, and continued the game. On the
last cast the trout came after the streamer with a rush and fell
all over himself trying to grab it. He was either a crazy fish or
not as patient as I was. There would be some satisfaction in
knowing which.

Finding a trout that is already excited, without benefit of a
marabou, is sheer luck. But even sane fish are inclined to go off
their balance when the stork feather sets to work. Of course, it
isn't a cure-all—but when fishing gets tough, give me a marabou
every time.

I must amend a sentence on Page 181. Keeping "your rod parallel to the surface" when retrieving a streamer fly is the way most of us learned to fish these feathery foolers. But somewhere along the way during the past twenty years I've discovered that by lowering the tip to and sometimes just under the surface I have better control. This beats mending for slack in cross-stream casts and gives the fly a much more lifelike swim. In fact it's applicable to still water, especially if you are fishing from a boat, which elevates the rod even more. When streamer fishing, that critical three of four feet of slack line between your tip and the surface won't permit a very short, natural pulsing action in the fly, literally inch-long darts and pauses. Also, you are in "hand" contact with the fly, and the ratio of hooked fish to strikes is much higher when the rod tip is lower. This of course doesn't apply to that odd occasion when you want to skip the fly over the surface.

I haven't changed my mind about marabou streamers, although some new patterns have been developed (such as the Marabou Muddler and Dave Whitlock's Multicolored Marabou series) which have replaced some of my old favorites. But despite pattern the premium is still on the skill of the angler. Not long ago I fished with Raul Miramon in the Limay River of Argentina, where he beached a 29½-pound brown trout on a streamer fly. The fly was a caricature, about the size of a small feather duster with a wing made of a variety of hackle feathers—no two alike. As

Raul explained, he just used up whatever was left on his tying bench. Needless to say, streamer flies do not produce under all conditions, but in reviewing the winners in the last twenty years of *Field & Stream's* Fly-Casting Division there's no question that they take the biggest fish in almost every category. Of course the entire art form of saltwater fly fishing is based on the streamer and bucktail, even though the wing may be modified to a short length as in bonefish patterns.

CHAPTER XI

The Wet Fly

PERHAPS THE clear water had fooled me; perhaps I only thought the fly was swinging deep. There are many things about which I could say "perhaps," but a bead-body fly, a Dusty Miller, did the work. I could feel it bounce along the gravel. The fly had already passed several large salmon in the first few feet, and when it reached the sluice I was ready to pick up and cast again. A huge steel-gray form rose from the depths of the hole, not rushing to the fly, but coming gently and deliberately to take and turn downward with the confidence of an old fish.

I saw him many times during the next hour—in the air, around my feet, over the tops of rapids, and resting in back waters just a few yards away. Once, after a particularly hard bout he came to the rod's pressure, and I clawed desperately at the back of his head—it was much too big to get a grip on, and with each thrust at his gill covers the massive body would quiver and bolt away. I tried circling him, and we ran round and round as I snatched at his tail, but hand-tailing a steelhead is like grabbing a greased watermelon. Nowhere could I find a beach, not one little gravel bar, for the Stamp flows bank-full, and even the banks are hidden by down timber. A sickening feeling came over me. He was a giant steelhead, and for that frantic moment I wanted him badly. The rod, the line, the leader, all the object of past losses, functioned perfectly. In time I began wishing the leader would break or the fly would pull out—and it happened as I wished it.

I went back to the sluice later and caught a steelhead of about 12 pounds. The bead-body fly was everything Jim Pray had predicted. Simply because it bounced on the stream bottom when nothing else would, I caught fish. Here was a perfect case of deep enough—a term that sums up wet fly fishing completely. But what *is* deep enough, and where is it? The veteran steelhead angler seeks to get his lure in the downward suction of eddies and whirlpools; he estimates the probable drift and mends his line to delay drag and swim the fly deeper. He knows that deep enough means brushing the bottom in meat-and-potatoes steelheading. Still his fly may lack three inches in its flight through holding water; it may bounce through an eddy and ride five inches higher than the fish cares to move, or it may sink ten inches in shallow water when the steelhead wants it in the surface film.

At the other extreme, a few days after my gravel bouncing catch, I fished the Ash River, a tributary to the Stamp. The Ash is a normal stream in most respects—the only elements lacking are fishermen and roads. Of the many things I remember about it, one was the long walk across the burn and down timber, the long trek down to the Junction Pool. I knew the pools where the steelhead were supposed to be. Between each one I fished long shallow riffles, perhaps no more than a foot deep, running very fast with a broken surface that belied the presence of fish. Certainly it was no place for a steelhead. I took it for granted that migrants, having come this far, would be resting in the slow water. After working two pools I turned to the riffs again, not because I wanted to, but simply because I found wading easier than climbing through timber to make my way downstream.

Where the first fish came from is hard to say. The water was about ten inches deep, flat, open, and seemingly devoid of life. The fly was dragging across the surface about forty feet below me as I climbed over a sunken brush pile. Suddenly, the rod tip snapped downward, the reel grated, gear against gear, and a heavy bright fish leaped into the air—purely an accident. It was in the run above the Falls Pool, and I had about two hundred yards to hold the trout in before he'd made the lip of swift water. The fact that the water was so shallow appeared to be in my favor as the steelhead jumped and fell like a wild animal, never finding a strong current to put his weight against. A half hour later I weighed and released my first steelie from the Ash—14 pounds.

By nightfall I had taken and released nine fish, the smallest weighing a shade under 8 pounds—all in shallow water on a surface-dragging wet fly. Casting and drifting the fly in the usual fashion resulted in absolutely nothing, but a slow surface retrieve brought smashing strikes with fair regularity. That in essence is the picture of wet fly fishing, whether the game is steelhead, bass, or trout; it is a method where the slightest difference in the depth of a drifting fly will influence your success.

The wet fly has been in use ever since fly fishing began. Oddly enough, there are fewer competent wet-fly anglers on the stream today than there are dry-fly adherents, even though the floating fly is a comparatively modern development. There were probably more skilled sunken fly men in the years before 1860, because from that year hence, a gentleman angler floated his feathers. We all realize a fair degree of success with the wet fly, but for the most part, the trout caught are in the law-of-averages anyhow, and would have swallowed a well-cast collar button. The basic questions—upstream or down, nymph imitation or minnow—are not easy to answer, for the game is played below the surface, the trout are out of sight, and the fly is out of touch.

We have seen that the dry fly is usually fished upstream, or slightly quartering, and allowed to drift in a natural manner. A wet fly on the other hand, is fished in a number of ways, and the method selected is dependent on stream conditions. But the chief difference is that the wet fly is usually given some motion by the angler—by stripping the line in short jerks or working the rod tip to make the fly look alive. One of the most common approaches is for the angler to wade into the head of a pool and cast his wet fly across stream, sending it swimming down with the current, and when drag sets in he can bring it to life by imparting some motion with his rod tip. He can fish the fly "dead" as it swings downstream to imitate a drifting nymph or drowned insect and work it in erratic strokes and darts coming back to appear as some minnow, shrimp, or fly. Using a somber pattern such as the Hare's Ear, Leadwing Coachman, Gray Hackle Yellow, or Mallard Quill, he can imitate anything—going down and coming back. Fancy patterns which bear hardly any resemblance to insect forms, such as the Butcher, Silver Doctor, and Alexandria, are more likely to make their kill on the retrieve, as the bright colors simulate trout and salmon fry.

Anglers who have difficulty with downstream wet fly fishing invariably spook their fish by dragging the fly back in a steady movement. This is unnatural, as none of the trout's forage swims in that manner. One of the most successful ways of fishing a wet fly in still water for instance, is to make a long cast and let the fly sink for several seconds before starting the retrieve. With the rod tip held low, strip the line in short, quick pulls. Underwater, the fly will be making a series of short dashes; the soft hackle opening and closing adds to the illusion of a minnow or swimming insect pushing against the current. Most of us learn to fish the wet fly in this fashion simply because it's the easiest way of getting a few fish, but there's no doubt that we would pass up a great many trout if we stuck to the downstream course.

In low, clear water, for instance, usually the most effective method is to cast upstream and slightly across, allowing the fly to submerge and drift back with the current. Naturally, you must retrieve the slack line with your left hand, but be careful not to disturb the natural motion of the fly. Trout come out of seemingly barren water, darting from under a rock or bank to take the free-moving fly even when other methods have failed. Since there are so many ways of fishing a wet fly, it is wise to switch from one to the other until the fish respond. How this works in practice may be illustrated in these two experiences.

I have waded the lower Beaverkill many times without finding or seeing a trout. The trout are there, but they are few, and here, as on many heavily fished Eastern rivers, they find a perfect camouflage among bass and chubs. This is tough water to fish because it's broad, open, and very uncertain. The August day I have in mind ran true to form for the first few hours. It was hot and sticky. Insects buzzed around my head, and often I had to stop casting to swat the deer flies off my hands. Even the chubs were conspicuous by their absence, but I stuck to my labors with determination. I fished long casts, dead-drift across and up, then jiggled the flies and bounced them on the bottom. A bucktail didn't help, aside from one smallmouth of 7 or 8 inches.

The first big pool up is a long stretch of dead water that runs against the railroad bank. It is deep, clear and shadeless. A few large boulders are seated on the railroad side, but aside from this cover, it is barren water. I fished the bank carefully, covering the pool from end to end and side to side. Upon reaching the riffle at the head of the pool, I lengthened my leader from eleven to fifteen feet with a fine tippet and tied on a very small wet fly of some kind. The leader didn't cast properly with my line, but I was less interested in casting now.

I worked out sufficient line to get the fly settled with the current, and then started to walk back downstream, pausing frequently to twitch the fly over some likely place. Once in a while I picked up for a new cast to cover a pocket or eddy that I couldn't touch with the drift, but for the most part the fly was fishing all the time. By wading in midstream, it was necessary to drift forty or fifty feet of line below to keep from stepping on the fish. Even at that distance I could see the river bottom quite clearly now.

The first chub broke off because of my striking too hard. On the next I found that all the force needed was in slowly elevating my rod tip and tightening on him. I lost a half dozen flies before a trout came up, but he was a strong fish of better than a pound and I felt pleased with myself when I landed him. Needless to say, it was enjoyable fishing, so much so that I covered the whole flat all the way down to the Junction Pool at the East Branch, a mile of big water.

The trout were lying wherever there was a submerged boulder or slab of rock that would offer some cover. This was a factor that I had never considered before. Previously I had just accepted the big river as one would look at a saucer of milk—I knew it had a bottom and took its contours for granted—but never really saw how it was formed. Fishing the drift downstream gave me that chance. Going up I was more concerned with wading and casting, the flies coming back so fast that they never really fished at all. Now I could see the pot-holes, the rock formations, and gravel bars. There was plenty of time to play the fly over what I knew to be holding water.

By working the lure temptingly over the widely scattered places that could hold trout, I was bound to score a good average. The fly that spends the better part of a day in the water is certain to give satisfaction. This in effect is the approach to wet fly fishing—know the stream bottom and design a method to exploit it. So now we find that we cannot say downstream or upstream alone, for there are methods within the method, and these are what pay off. While the Beaverkill was ripe for downstream fishing in late summer, the following spring on opening day I went to another Catskill stream and picked up where I had left off.

In general, I believe the downstream method is more convenient, practical, and successful. This is particularly the case during the early weeks of the season when the water is high. Also, casting up, or up and across, on a fast and rocky stream, the current in many places takes the fly downstream at a pace which makes it difficult for even the strongest and most active fish to connect with the artificial. But when fishing downstream, casting across and allowing the current to swing the fly around to a point directly below the fisherman, it is possible for the angler to guide his fly at a restrained pace over the most likely-looking spots. Thus the fly is more effectively advertised.

Fishing downstream was the easiest way to start out that morning. The Chichester was flowing clear and bankfull, and because of the steep gradient of the river bed, going down was less tiring. I tied on a pair of wet flies, a Mallard Quill and a Leadwing Coachman for the dropper, and started combing the pocket water. Here and there I would step into a pot-hole and get pushed along with the current, but the stream was interesting and full of promise.

I caught five or six small rainbows in the backwaters, but nothing came to my flies from the main channel, or even from the deep pockets behind boulders. After an hour had passed, the Chichester still hadn't showed me an adult fish. Upon reaching the iron bridge, I got out of the stream and crossed to the other side. The bank I had been wading would be for a left-handed caster going upstream, and obviously I needed every advantage I could muster.

Facing the current was hard work at first, but I found by wading in the back eddies from boulder to boulder I could concentrate on my fishing. I would cover the eddy first with as many casts as the water required and then moved forward, reaching for the next above. At about the third boulder a rainbow picked the Mallard Quill from the bottom and swam off quickly, setting the hook. Even as the trout turned, a slightly smaller rainbow dashed after the Leadwing and struck sharply. This is the only double I have ever scored in civilized waters.

The method to use soon made itself apparent. By fishing the flies as deep and as slowly as possible—not ordinary slow, but slow to the point of their being fished as bait—the Chichester gave me a limit of fine trout. Each cast was an occupation. The flies would drop behind a boulder, the line bellying with slack, and from there on the game was to see how long I could keep the flies in one place. The cast that gave the Leadwing and Mallard time to examine all the crevices and rocks along the bottom of the eddy would be taken greedily. Even the main channel became an active hunting ground, provided I could mend the cast to work deep enough.

As experience has shown, the "dead area"—that thin layer of almost currentless water along boulder-strewn bottoms—holds and protects the springtime trout. Even minnows and fry can be found in what appears to be a torrent of racing water when viewed from the surface. Nature keeps the trout's food conveniently at hand. Aquatic food in the Chichester was plentiful, and the fish had no need to come up in heavier currents to stab at stray nymphs—or anglers' flies.

Only a deep-fished lure will take trout at a time like this, which accounts for "unusual" early-season catches taken on minnows and worms. The downstream wet fly fisher can't begin to touch the dead area, not even with his weighted nymphs; the fly or nymph is buoyed up by a dragging line and is played in strong current. In less violent water the weighted lure may serve well, but spring is seldom gentle. A trout would have the chest expansion of an eel if continually forced to fight currents in the search for food. This is sometimes the case after a severe winter when the stream bed has been scoured by floods and ice; the nymphs and larvae are carried off and the trout of April is in poor condition. As with everything in fishing, it is dangerous to generalize. It has been noticed that in some streams food production is increased after flooding. Much depends on the type of stream bottom and the predominant food forms.

It does hold true, however, that the early-season trout is seldom an active hunter, as the lower water temperatures prevailing at this time decrease his energy requirements and retard digestion. The available bottom organisms are usually sufficient to keep him happy. You can check this by examining the stomach contents of trout taken in early season when the weather is still cold. Much of the larvae and easily digestible organisms in the stomach will still be alive. I find this a more reliable guide than my stream thermometer when I can't make up my mind about depth and method.

There was a generation of anglers on the Catskill streams at the turn of the century that fished three and four wet flies at a time—all the time. They would make their casts across and downstream, then skip the flies back over the surface; this was a simple, practical way of telling the trout that here was something to eat. The effectiveness of such a direct approach was lost as each crop of new anglers appeared—the brown trout replaced the brook trout, and the fly-fishing lore of chalk streams clouded American waters. People were now educated to using a single floating fly, and in this pursuit of classic form they forgot the simple tricks that filled baskets a decade before.

In modern trouting, I'm inclined to believe that one catches as many or more fish by using only one fly and concentrating on working it just right. This is especially true of dry fly fishing. But all fly fishing is not devoted to the trout, the dry fly, and ideal conditions. A great deal of time is spent casting one fly in water where two would be more appropriate. Occasionally you'll find somebody fishing two floaters or a pair of wet flies on one cast, and less frequently you'll meet a three and four wet-fly angler. The apparent reason for fishing more than one fly is to give the trout a choice—just as the strap artists did in Stewart's day. There is sufficient evidence in angling literature to indicate that it's a sound thesis; we read of anglers who used a brown hackle every time, whether it was used as a tail fly or a dropper. In more than one instance the angler has used a quartet of flies, and no matter where the killing pattern was hidden, his trout would find it. I have never experienced this kind of selectivity, but I have managed to creel a few good fish by using three wet flies when a single fly went untouched. When fished together, a number of flies can be as deadly an attractor to trout as a herring "grapevine" is to tuna fish. H. A. Rolt tells us that professional fishermen on the Tweed and Clyde use nine flies on their leaders, and that French anglers use from eight to ten gaudy patterns for fishing on the river Ain. Personally I have no desire to throw such a string of flies in my trout waters, but the use of two- and three-fly casts is an important part of practical angling. You can catch fish that wouldn't otherwise be caught.

Two wet flies can be exceptionally good. On our Catskill streams we cast this rig across current, and, holding the rod high, strip the line back with definite short strokes. The slim form of a sunken pattern skims through the surface rather than skipping over it, both flies making a faint V-shaped wake, similar to the trail left by beetles and water boatmen. By holding the rod up, most of the line will be off the water, and a very lifelike retrieve is possible. This is most effective in evening stream-fishing and was the cast that made old Pop Robbins famous on the Beaverkill. Pop was accused of many kinds of witchcraft in his day, but actually his phenomenal successes were based on this direct approach. Over on the Neversink, where currents are stronger and the water bigger, John Pope made his reputation by skimming three big wet flies into the choppers of a waiting trout. With the resignation that is the final courage of old age, Uncle John used a single dry fly just before he died. He reported that the method had "interesting possibilities."

There is a variation of the two wet-fly technique that I call *diving-and-bobbing*. The chief virtue of this method is that it brings up trout in perfectly dead water. No doubt somebody was fishing this way long before I, but I discovered this two-fly trick quite accidentally. As we all learn, lake fly fishing is difficult. I think the chief reason for this is that artificial flies have very little inherent action, and there's practically nothing the angler can do to simulate life without the help of a current. We can jerk streamers and wet flies through the water and make a fair score and twitch a dry fly over rising fish, but most people will agree that the quality of the catch depends on how actively the fish are feeding. If the water is glassy, the sun bright, and our fish well fed, each offering is going to be inspected closely, because the trout doesn't have to act quickly. There's no current to take his food away.

I was fishing a small Adirondack pond one afternoon, letting my canoe drift with the breeze. There were a few trout rising from time to time, and I managed to catch one of them on a wet fly. Thinking that the pattern was wrong I tied on a dropper strand and a small, sparsely dressed Gray Hackle. Because it was fresh, and because the hackle was stiff, the new fly wouldn't sink —it simply relaxed on the surface. I gave the line a few pulls to get the fly under, but each time it bobbed up again. After the fourth or fifth pull a fat native smacked it. Obviously the action of the fly was important to the trout, so I cut off the tail fly and put on a similar Gray Hackle. From that moment on, business was brisk.

In the diving-and-bobbing method, it is important to use sparsely tied wet hackle patterns. I like a pair of No. 12 Gray Hackles with yellow bodies. After dousing them in dry-fly oil, shoot the cast out a good distance, and let them float quietly for several minutes. When trout are not actively feeding, the quiet float rarely draws a strike, but I suspect that any nearby fish might be looking at the flies. Now take the cast back in foot-long pulls—the flies dive and bob alternately, an action that no amount of rod work can duplicate. Obviously, you can do the same thing with a single fly and catch fish. But the two-fly cast has always been more productive for me, and I think this is because the trout are given twice the incentive to commence eating.

One of the most important skills in using two flies or more is to make a proper leader. The leader can't be too light, and the dropper strands must be tied properly to keep them from tangling. There are a number of knots you can use, but they all slip down the leader sooner or later, so it's a good idea to tie them just above one of the taper knots and pull until secure. However, I would suggest making dropper strands when you build your leaders, or buy leaders with droppers already made. I use an extra long length of the heavier strand when two strands are joined in making the taper. Whether you use the blood knot or the barrel knot, when the knot is finally formed and the stem end is pulled through, it's an easy matter to pull out another eight or ten inches. The extra length cannot be pulled from the already formed knot, but should be allowed for when you begin making the tie. If, for instance, my taper calls for a 20-inch strand of .012 and then a 20-inch strand of .010, I use about 28 inches of the .012, which gives me an 8-inch dropper strand. The dropper should always be of the heavier diameter between any two sizes so that it will stand away from the leader. For the same reason you cannot use too large a fly on the dropper, or the weight of the fly will cause a tangle every time.

In the matter of pattern, I have never found the need for exact imitation so great that a Hare's Ear would take fewer fish than something tied to imitate a submerged beetle. The form and substance of a sunken fly are deciding factors. True, if a trout were feeding on beetles, a fly so tied would inspire the angler's confidence. Yet a beetle imitation poorly fished would be looked upon with more suspicion by a trout than a poorly fished Hare's Ear which has no counterpart in the water to be compared with. I carry tinseled flies, and quill-bodied flies, but on the whole I favor a wet fly body tied from the underfur of polar bear or seal's fur. In the eyes of a trout, I think the furs are more translucent and lifelike in the water than many exact imitations which feature glossy quill segments and fine speckled tails. Most important to me is a long, soft hackle at the head of the fly to give the lure motion, and a heavy wire hook to insure fast sinking. The ideal wet fly is one which sinks immediately upon contact with the water and travels under the surface at all times. The best wet flies, therefore, are those which have heavy hooks and are lightly dressed. Many flies are encumbered with too much hackle, wing, and body. They can be improved by trimming off at least 50 per cent of the dressing. Strangely enough, such lures are often more attractive to the fish.

A classic example of the fur-bodied fly, and one that is most effective on big trout, is the Fledermouse. This pattern is literally tied with clumps of muskrat fur using both the underfur and guard hairs, and the result is a tufted, mousy-looking fly with a sparse gray squirrel wing. The late Jack B. Schneider of San Jose, California, originated this pattern in 1949, and since that time we've put the Fledermouse to many a test; in my own experience, the fly scored a good 40 per cent when used under appropriate conditions. Here's what Jack had to report:

> The Fledermouse is mainly a late evening and night fly. It is at its best from the time the bats put in their first appearance over the water and on into the night. That is how it received the name "Fledermouse." The pattern was conceived one rainy morning in August at Wade Lake, Montana. In its first season it was used over a period of six weeks for about three hours every evening. It proved to be a knockout.
>
> I recall one evening in particular when my wife and I were fishing with friends, Don and Dick Olson, two of West Yellowstone's best fly tiers and guides. Don and Dick fished marabou streamers which they considered tops for this piece of water. Wading and fishing the same stretch of water, the final score for two hours of casting was eleven fish for the Fledermouse and two on the marabou streamers. I was high man with six fish, landing only one out of three that took a chance on the Fledermouse. My wife beached five and had the largest fish taken that evening, a male brown that weighed four pounds. Only two of the eleven fish landed were under two pounds.
>
> Wade Lake holds three species of trout—browns, rainbow, and native cutthroat. The largest trout I beached during the six weeks

I used the fly last summer was no record breaker, but a male brown of five pounds, two ounces, can't be flipped over your shoulder either. I landed better than fifty that ran from three to four pounds, and quite a number from one-and-one-half to three pounds. On only five evenings during these six weeks did I fail to land a fish over two pounds. In all probability the Fledermouse must have had something to do with the amount and size of fish I was hooking. The majority of the time it had an edge on the other fly patterns that were being used in this water, and on more than one occasion it took two and sometimes three to one over any other pattern.

Now for the tying of the Fledermouse. I doubt if there is a more simple pattern to make. Try hook sizes one, two, or three, standard length and wire. I have even used No. 4 in 4X long shank, which really makes a mouthful. Secure your thread to the hook shank at the start of the bend. There is no tail so that eliminates all chance of fouling up that part of the fly. The body is muskrat fur, under hair and guard hairs combined. It is the guard hairs sticking out from the body that give it that tufted appearance. Don't pull them out.

It takes about three clumps of hair to make a body. To define a clump of hair? It's roughly the amount you can get hold of between thumb and index finger. Next, cut three clumps of muskrat fur off the piece of skin and lay them on your tying table, or on your leg, as I prefer to do it.

The fly is now as good as tied. Take hold of the tying silk you have already secured to the hook; lay the left index finger across the silk about four inches from the hook; then carry the silk around and over the finger back to the bend of the hook, and spiral the silk forward to within one-eighth inch of the eye of the hook. Make half hitch. You now have a four inch loop of tying silk attached to the hook just at the bend where you would tie on the tail if the pattern called for one. Your left index finger is still in the loop, holding it taut. Pick up the first clump of hair, holding it by the butts, and center it in the open end of the loop, then slide it down through the loop to the shank of the hook.

Take the second clump, insert in loop as before and slide down to within half an inch of the first clump. Now space the third and last clump of hair half an inch from the second clump. Now, with the thumb and forefinger of the right hand, take hold of the open end of the loop bringing the two strands of silk together. With the left hand attach hackle pliers to loose end of loop.

Keeping the loop taut, spread the hair evenly for about two inches between the strands of silk. Revolve the hackle pliers until you twist what resembles a rough, furry strand of chenille about two inches long. Wrap this around the shank of the hook almost to the eye, and tie it off. Tie on a grey squirrel tail wing, and you have a Fledermouse. Tying time approximately two to three minutes.

For years I looked around for a good shrimp imitation, a wet fly that would serve for tidal stream fishing where this food form is abundant. I suppose any number of brightly dressed flies could be mistaken for shrimp, but there is one pattern which really rates at the head of the list—the Horner Shrimp. Jack Horner and his shrimp fly need no introduction to most West Coast anglers. Both are recognized fish takers. This pattern is considered by many as the perfect shrimp imitation; at least results bear out this conclusion. It was developed on the Eel River in 1938, and since that time the dressing has been widely acclaimed up and down the coast.

Horner's shrimp fly was designed principally for fishing in and around salt water. Steelhead and salmon are extremely fond of shrimp and they often feed heavily on this food while in the lagoons and brackish water areas near the mouths of rivers. Although associated with steelhead, the fly will take any shrimp-feeding salt-water species. A size 4 is best for general use, but I have the shrimp tied on size 8 and 10 hooks for trout and panfish. The dressing deviates from the usual wet fly shape in that the brown bucktail "wing" is secured at the hook bend to form the back of the shrimp. The "tail" is simply an extension of the wing below the point where it was tied off. This gives the fly a shrimp-like curve, and the fat tinsel body which is padded with tying silk and wound with heavy silver provides the necessary bulk. A pale grayish-olive hackle at the head serves for legs. Light brown tying silk, the same color as the bucktail, is recommended because the silk shows not only at the head but on the hook bend as well.

In general, tidal fly-fishing is quite a dependable game, if the fish are about. Yet, in recalling many off days in the past, I'm inclined to believe that on occasion there is some kind of feed at the river mouths, perhaps microscopic in size, which diverts their attention. The abundance of small shrimp is often responsible for a difficult rise, but invariably a sparse pattern with a dash of orange in the wing hackle will score even if you don't have a shrimp imitation.

A trip I made several years ago for cutthroat trout is typical of those situations that remain for you to solve. It was a stream on the coast of British Columbia, and I couldn't get any information on the angling other than the fact that the tide-water section always produced trout. I knew from past experience that tidal cutthroats can be very difficult at times, and a knowledge of local conditions as to tides and feed is invaluable. So in lieu of anything else I worked on the assumption that cutthroats prefer dark-colored wet flies with some flash of tinsel in the pattern.

The tide was running out when I arrived at the river mouth and saw what I had come for—cutthroats. Not one or two, or a dozen, but at least a hundred, and perhaps more. They were small fat fish. None would go much more than a pound. But they flashed and darted like bars of gold in the green water, feeding and moving slowly toward the flow of the current. I found that I could wade very close to the trout without scaring them. It was easy wading on the hard yellow sand and a short cast to reach them. A Silver Brown for the point fly and a Butcher for the dropper—that seemed good, and I was confident of quick results. Making the necessary motions, I lengthened a cast and let the flies settle.

Ten minutes later I changed flies, and five minutes later changed again. A small fish turned over once and flashed below a Hare's Ear, but that was all. I was using a light tippet, and the turbidity of the water didn't seem to demand anything finer; so I cut off the dropper, thinking that the added weight somehow spoiled my cast. The cutthroats worked away from my reach several times, and I found it necessary to wade back and forth to keep up with their movements—changing, wading, and casting. The tide turned and began racing back to the river mouth. The fish continued to rise, just making small dimples on the surface, but soon the rushing water obliterated their reflections, and I was forced to make for shore.

This was the exceptional day, to be sure, for I can remember other days on other waters when the cutthroat tore into the fly with reckless abandon. But the trout I pursued up and down the tidal bars that day were hunting something far less obvious, and, judging from the slowness of their rise, it was an almost stationary food. Each time the trout wouldn't take, the same characteristic rise was apparent. Apparently the fly was deep enough but the angler not wise enough—there was no compromise there.

The most important thing I've learned about wet-fly fishing during the past twenty years is that two and three fly combinations greatly increase the odds in taking trout. That "old-fashioned" Catskill style of John Pope is as effective today as it was in the 1930s. This of course is nothing new in Europe where the multi-fly cast is centuries old. While fishing the limestone lakes of Ireland, which still enjoy what must be the world's most prolific mayfly emergences, I have had trout come to the same pattern again and again whether it was tied on as the tail fly, dropper, or hand fly. One of the largest Eastern brown trout I've caught in recent years, a 7-pound 10-ounce fish from the upper Connecticut River, came to a three-fly cast of Dark Cahills. Earlier that day the trout were showing a preference for that pattern, so it was a logical choice. Apparently H. A. Rolt's advice is still in favor, as I met an angler on the Buna River in Yugoslavia a few seasons ago who was using a dozen flies on one cast and very successfully. He was catching trout from under my feet. This I soon learned is a common method in that country. Personally I find three flies a happy maximum; on the retrieve you can get a nice surface skipping action in the hand and dropper flies. The flies must be small, however, no larger than a No. 14 and preferably a No. 16 or No. 18, and dressed rather sparsely. This usually brings good results on our western rivers during the summer months.

Michael Rogan (Ballyshannon Co., Donegal, Ireland) purveys already mounted three-fly "casts" tied on fine nylon in familiar American patterns. These are handy to stock and can be simply joined to the butt section of your leader. Rogan is one of the world's great fly dressers and his patterns are properly sparse.

CHAPTER XII

Panfish

THE PANFISH and I have always been at odds with each other; in fact, fishing for them is reminiscent of certain popular ballads which depict in a poetic frenzy the virtues of a vagrant Juliet who (except for yours and mine, dear reader) was probably as ugly as a mud turtle. But now that the fair one is paddling in somebody else's pond, our balladier wants sweet Lulu Belle back. This ordinary account of angling has no quarrel with the way of love. It is merely mentioned here to point out that little fish as a rule, and panfish in particular, have their redeeming qualities. While I thoroughly dislike having pickerel swallow all my baits when I'm bass fishing—most bass fishermen do—I have been known to hunt them tirelessly after the bass season has closed and the cold bite of winter is at my neck. He is the last fish to hit a fly before a heavy blanket of ice keeps us apart, so in this late hour I am just fickle enough to write a crystal melody to belie his duck-billed face. I will even pursue bream into the buck-brush. The perch and the crappie can be bright and spirited, so if you have followed this weak philosophical thread, obviously the thrill of pursuit must depend on the relative position of the angler.

About the time of our first snowfall I usually have a day of pickerel fishing—not through the ice—but in one of our ponds or creeks that hasn't frozen over. We have a number of such places locally, and being at a period when pickerel are most active, these open waters provide delightful sport with the fly rod. Everything may seem gray and bare then—the fields, the

214

hedges, farm houses, and fences—even the lake is no more than an empty amusement where bull frogs once played. But if you invade the shoreline in warm waders, waving a big, bright streamer for that touch of color our winter fish like, angling undergoes a profound metamorphosis. The pickerel are apt to be larger (I have taken them up to four pounds in early December) and certainly more pugnacious. Being a weed fish, they normally forage along the shore line growths of lily pads, rushes, and tree stumps. Here their coloring blends perfectly with the background, and the pickerel can lie motionless waiting for schools of minnows, baby perch, or sunfish to wander by. Once the minnow gets within range, the pickerel makes a slashing attack which often kicks up a disturbance for yards around. It doesn't make much difference how shallow the water might be; almost any weedy cove that holds baitfish will harbor pickerel. Of course in winter the weeds are almost gone, and the forage species are both scarce and inactive. This condition makes the streamer fly doubly attractive. The fish hit without hesitation and frequently run and jump in great style. I can still see Dan Todd blowing snowflakes off his coat collar, feigning indifference to a wild-eyed pickerel as the fish seesawed his line under a log. Dan would never admit that fishing was fun after the mayfly season.

Panfish are made perfectly for the beginning fly-fisher. They can be found in almost any city park or in suburban places an hour away. At least two or three kinds can be caught all year round, and usually panfish can be taken with such short casts that they offer a perfect course of instruction to the novice. In some waters they will prove very timid, thereby adding the first ingredient to the making of a skilled caster. Most of them will rise to anything that looks good to eat, and they come in such a way that the angler can see clearly how a fish feeds and why the fly was accepted. Too, they are found in large numbers, so the novice has many fish to practice on—a condition that does

not exist among nobler game fish. And in the proper setting, a
school of white perch, for instance, can offer many hours of
fishing pleasure. I remember one day in particular on Messalonskee Lake in Maine after a slow morning with the brook trout.

While crossing the lake on my way back to camp, I noticed
a disturbance inshore, a faint swirl, followed by another deeper
swirl. In a matter of minutes my rod was shaking to the strain
of a powerful fish, a deep-boring, head-shaking scrap, not unlike
the work of a heavy squaretail. It took about five minutes to
bring the fish to net, but this turned out to be a short time for
two-and-a-half pounds of white perch. For the rest of the afternoon I followed the school, sometimes losing their location but
always finding them again when silver flashed against the pale
sand. By nightfall, thirty-odd perch had come to net—one of the
finest day's fly fishing I've ever had. Panfishing isn't always like
that, naturally. It just happens that Messalonskee is productive
perch water; in fact, this is where the world's record of 4¾
pounds was caught in July, 1949.

It has been my observation that geography makes the panfish
addict. Take Ketona Lake near Tarrant, Alabama, as an example.
Ketona has become a piscatorial landmark for the panfish crowd.
Given a fair day with the bream on the prowl, you're apt to
come up with a hat full of records. In one season Ketona gave
up a 3-pound 2-ounce pumpkinseed, a 2-pound 12-ounce bluegill, and a 2-pound 10-ounce redear sunfish, to mention a few.
That's more weight than a lot of eastern troutsters tuck in the
oven. But while the South has fat sunfish, the northern talent can
fly-fish through the ice. An ice fly looks like almost any standard
pattern of wet fly, except that you clamp a split shot to the shank
of the hook to give it weight, before dressing the fly. It calls for
soft hackles or a marabou wing, and gantron floss in red or
yellow makes a body that glows brightly in the dimly-lighted
world of an ice-covered pond. The fisherman uses a short, limber stick, such as the tip section of an old fly rod, and a light

line, preferably nylon monofilament. He sits by a hole in the ice, patiently jiggling the fly up and down in the water. Sometimes the perch or bluegill grabs the fly on the upstroke, sometimes on the downdrop. It's fun, it solves the annual problem of getting bait during cold weather—and, more important, it takes fish. So, geographically speaking, the panfish game ranges from hot to cold, and the possibilities are unlimited.

Panfishing rises from humble ponds and bayous, where the prize may be a fat copper-nose bream or a bluegill sunfish, to the historic waters of the Seine, where the prize can be a silver trophy worth thousands of dollars. France is the only nation in the world that respects its panfishing champions in the grand manner. This fabulous prize comes after countless elimination contests throughout the provinces, with as many as ten thousand entrants at the start. The finals of the Violet Byrrh Tournament are held in Paris, where some two hundred men, women, and children swim their baits for perch, whitefish, and anything that comes along. The average catch is about the size of an exhausted sardine—but they're weighed and measured with the same attention given a bluefin tuna at the international cup matches.

England is not immune to "match" fishing. The 1949 competition, for instance, drew 924 anglers for the championship. This group was broken into 77 teams competing for the N.F.A. Challenge Cup, the Peek Cup, two other cups, and a flock of medals. The anglers fished like machines from the moment the opening rocket went up, casting for bream along ten miles of river bank. Twenty thousand fish were caught in five hours' fishing, and each angler had twenty yards of water to work in.

Geography isn't the whole story, of course. Some of us get bitten by the light-tackle bug and need a dependable species to work over; this excludes most of the larger game fish in civilized waters. Trout and bass are too scarce for the angler to waste time covering long reaches of water with delicate tackle. Panfish, on the other hand, are abundant and always willing to take a lure. The feeding cycle and habits of each species vary from one water to the next, presenting just as many tactical problems as we find on the trout stream. Some generalizations can be made, but by and large the angler has to be flexible in his approach.

I bought one of those matchstick-sized fly rods a number of years ago, thinking that it would add more sport to my trouting. This fragile wand proved inadequate for long hours of difficult casting, but there was a sense of pleasure in its use—on quiet ponds and creek backwaters where the bluegills live. But when fishing conditions are going to require my using heavy lures such as a spinner-and-fly combination, or if I have to buck strong winds when casting on open lakes, obviously the light rod is not a proper tool. Often I go to the other extreme and use a bass rod. However, heavy tackle was not intended for hunting the panfish on a lazy summer day, and whenever possible I use the little rod, even though some of my versatility is lost.

One summer I spent an afternoon on a small brackish pond on Long Island. This spot is full of white perch—fish that average about a half-pound in size—and down near the outlet where a broad salt-water creek is formed, I located a school of perch that looked to be twice as big. I pushed through the swale and waded for a short distance along a sand-bar. The first fish took a small silver-bodied wet fly and shot across stream into the main flow of current. The rod whipped into a tight little bow and for several minutes I had my hands full. For an hour the school stayed in my vicinity, and when the action ceased I waded back toward the pond, casting as I went. The last cast below the spillway erupted in a savage strike, and I was fast to a smallmouth bass— one of those unearned dividends that the panfisher is sometimes blessed with. My bass wasn't a big one by bait-casting standards, but played against the slender bamboo I had occasion to use every trick in the books to wear him down.

The white perch is bass-like in appearance, with a deeply

notched dorsal fin between the spines and rays, but connected by a very low membrane. Adults have a dark green back, silvery or light olive below. Young fish show dusky vertical bars above and slightly below the lateral line, but these markings are absent in older fish. Fresh-water populations are darker than the perch from brackish or tidal waters. The average size is about one-half pound, but under proper food conditions, the maximum size is thought to be about six pounds. The principal foods of white perch are nymphs, insect larvae, and water fleas. Minnows, small fish, and crustaceans form the smallest part of the diet, which is undoubtedly because of the perch's habit of feeding along the bottom in deep water where insect forms are most abundant. Large white perch will feed almost exclusively on fingerling game fish and minnows when they can get them. So a small spinner-and-fly combination is the most effective artificial lure for deep or shallow water fishing.

If you have no white perch to practice on, there may be some yellows near-by. I think the word "practice" is amiss here because this panfish frequently takes a dim view of the most polished performance. The yellow perch is also known by the names of racoon perch, jack perch, ring perch, American perch, and red perch. This fish varies greatly in color, but the pronounced color pattern of dark vertical bars from the back to below the middle of the sides is unmistakable. The upper fins are dusky, the lower fins orange or bright red. The mouth contains many small teeth, but no large canine or tearing teeth. This distinguishes it from the young walleyed pike, the only other fish which it may resemble. The profile of the head of the yellow perch is concave above the eyes, causing a humped outline just before the beginning of the dorsal fin. The average size of the yellow perch is small, often less than a half-pound, but in large bodies of water where food is suitable, yellow perch will reach a weight of two or three pounds. Yellow perch are almost wholly carnivorous, eating the young of other fishes, minnows, and crayfish. They bite readily on minnows and worms, and owing to their schooling habits which are retained throughout life, large numbers are easily caught. The best perch lakes are those which produce good smallmouth bass fishing—where there are extensive areas of submerged vegetation and considerable areas of rocky shore line. Yellow perch also feed on insects and insect larvae, but only when insect forms are at a peak of abundance. Actually, my best perch fishing has been more by chance than intent, like that day on Seneca Lake.

Seneca is a vast and complicated body of water. There are at least a dozen species of fish in the lake, and each has its period of abundance. Among greater fishes, the lake holds some very large yellow perch. I have caught them up to 2½ pounds and have seen much larger ones drifting under the surface on hot summer days. But there is also good smallmouth bass fishing, and being the "game" species, my tackle has always been dictated by the whims of bass. Now the habits and habitat of yellow perch and smallmouth bass are the same, so during the years I used bait-casting tackle on Seneca, only four or five heavy perch hit a pearl spoon intended for the smallmouths. If bass baits were an attraction to large perch, I think I should have caught a hundred times that number, but the perch is of a different temperament—slow and calculating. The lure he takes with confidence is a tiny one that he can study for some time. When he decides everything is in order, he seizes it with a rush. I am speaking now of the older yellow perch, not the infant fish, who are guided solely by their appetites. No bait-casting lure is qualified for this angling.

So the last trip to Seneca was a two-rod affair—a hot July afternoon, with insects blowing out over the lake. My fly rod was set up and ready for use, but I put it aside in order to get at the bass. I snapped on a deep-running plug and, with my boat drifting slowly along the ledges, began to catch fish. These smallmouths rest deep, and each cast required a long wait until the plug found a proper level. While sinking a cast, I happened to see a school of perch moving across the stern. There began one of the fastest sessions of perch-catching imaginable. The fish were coming to a raft of bees. These heavily laden insects seldom make a successful journey across the lake, and July perch roam far and wide to find a windrow of half-sunk bees. The fly rod was armed with a Brown Bivisible, and in one hour I had taken twenty-odd perch, weighing up to 2½ pounds. I kept five of the largest, and when the fish moved out of range I went back to my bass fishing. No more perch appeared that day, nor did I see any during the next few days. Migratory schools are not the kind of fish you can look for and reasonably expect to find.

Yellow perch are so definite in their schooling habits that University of Wisconsin scientists recently discovered that perch spend their nights asleep on the lake bottom near shore after making their daily migration from deep water. According to Professor Hasler, perch lose their schooling instinct at night when they can no longer see each other. It was this habit of quietly blending into the bottom that aroused the scientists' curiosity—because on the echo-sounding oscilloscope it seemed as though the perch disappeared. A diver sent below at night with a flashlight found thousands of perch on the bottom. When they were disturbed by the flashlight they would move just out of the brightest beam and sink again to the bottom.

Pre-dawn observations show that the perch remain in the same spot throughout the night. At daybreak they rise from the bottom and congregate into schools. Shortly after sunrise they move back into deeper water. In parts of the lake that are shallow, the perch have no need to migrate shoreward at night, according to Hasler, and the fish in shallow-water schools simply sink to the bottom when it gets dark.

Aside from their schooling habits, there is a definite feeding cycle which makes the big ones alternately abundant and scarce. The first chance comes in the latter part of May on waters having a large hatch of mayflies. Yellow perch will gorge themselves on the emerging insects when the nymphal skins drift on the surface. This lasts for a period of a week or ten days. If the hatch is a big one, the larger perch will feed night and day, and you can tab some really fast fishing. The next feeding situation suitable for the dry fly comes with the flying ant hatch in mid-June. Ants are not aquatic insects, but they go through a brief winged stage in which they swarm over the water in great clouds. This may occur for only two or three days, and then surface action stops. The third surface period comes during the bee migration in July. This is the best dry-fly opportunity in northern New York waters such as Lake Ontario and the Finger Lakes; the heavily laden bees, unable to cross the lake, fall to the surface where big schools of yellow perch are waiting.

The techniques of fly fishing for panfish are fairly routine in application. None of the pan species is fast on its fins, and in general it seems best to work the fly slowly. With the dry fly, for instance, make as long a cast as possible if you're not aiming at a rising fish, and let the lure sit for ten or fifteen seconds before retrieving. The retrieve should be made in short, halting steps, giving the fish plenty of time to get off the bottom and look the feathers over. Many anglers are inclined to work too fast, and often the slightest disturbance will put the big ones down. The wet fly should be fished in much the same manner, the only difference being that a longer time should be allowed before starting the retrieve to get the fly as deep as possible. The natural path of insect food in a lake is from bottom to top—unless you are actually fishing the surface when bees or ants are blowing on the water.

One of my favorite panfish lakes is heavily wooded, with the exception of the southeast side, where the shore is bordered by a large meadow. On days when there's a good wind blowing out of the south, that end of the pond gets a liberal dose of grasshoppers and crickets tossed on the surface. Sometimes it seems that every crappie in the lake moves into the meadow cove. When these flashy gamesters go surface-hunting the water fairly boils with rising fish. Both the grasshoppers and crickets move across the water in short jerks, and any small hackle pattern or, preferably, sedge pattern fished in the same way will connect instantly. There are a number of flies on the market, such as the Grasshopper Fly made by the Marathon Bait Company, or the Michigan Hopper made by Helen Shaw, which will do the same job.

You should keep a small stock of ringed-eye flies on hand, by the way, as the turned-down and turned-up eye in common use for wet flies and streamers have a tendency to cock at peculiar angles or else become ensnared on the spinner shaft. The flies should be sparsely dressed, tied on heavy-weight hooks. A thickly dressed bucktail, for instance, is inclined to buoy a small spinner near the surface, thereby reducing your field of play when working the lure. I like any of the polar bear patterns, especially the Woods Polar Bear, and as to bucktails, the Red-and-White, Black-and-White, and Mickey Finn rate among the best. In wet flies, the Black Gnat, Parmachene Belle, Gray Hackle, and Brown Hackle comprise a good color range, and I would suggest that you have your flies tied with chenille bodies rather than herl or silk, as they are most durable.

Crappie fishing has an element of attraction in that the fish are often very selective in their feeding. Neither the black nor white crappie is a lengthy fighter—unless you find them in a cold water stream, but they're handsome gamesters and excellent eating. Both species are generally found in warm, weedy water— the black being more inclined to creeks and large rivers and rarely found in big lakes. The white crappie averages a bit smaller than the black, but both will go over the two-pound mark, and a number have been reported in excess of three pounds. I'd guess that the overall average is about ¾ pounds when considering the waters from East Coast to West. They can be taken in large numbers though; it isn't unusual to catch thirty or forty good ones in some of our Southern lakes like Center Hill in Tennessee, where forage fish are particularly abundant.

Although the crappie feeds primarily on minnows, it can be a top-flight dry-fly fish in the right location. In some states, notably Wisconsin and Minnesota, where forage fish are abundant, the crappie feeds on minnows throughout the year—with much of the best fishing in the winter months. In regions like New England and the Appalachians the crappie is largely an insect hunter, as bait fish are relatively scarce in the waters where crappie have been planted. In Eastern waters, the odd fish will grab a streamer fly, but the best lure in my experience has been a small nymph. Like my friend Ben Robinson, I've found that nymphs are the most consistent lures for crappies, sunfish, and bluegills in still water. Ben favors a caddis nymph—one of those black and white chenille affairs that looks as if it were made out of an old pipe cleaner. Some shops sell them as grub or maggot imitations. At any rate, Ben is an authority on the subject of panfish, and in forty years of angling the sycamore runs of Ohio, his opinion has withstood the test of time.

There's a small unfished river not far from my town. As a matter of fact, it is within sight of our granite and steel towers. The state tried stocking it with trout for a number of years, but these thin-skinned aristocrats couldn't stand the place. That's how I came to find my sunfish factory. The stream is warm and slow flowing, with a muck bottom that is annually hidden by a heavy growth of chara weed. Near its source the stream is a bit colder, and long sweepers of watercress sway in the current, while brilliant-hued, fat little pumpkinseeds swing back and forth with the weeds, gulping the nymphs that shake loose.

When I first started fishing this stream a number of years ago, people crowded the banks, hoping to get a chance at the newly stocked trout. When the stocking was discontinued, the mob vanished. The brand of angling that remains is far more attractive from a fly-fishing standpoint. I rarely meet more than three or four anglers on this stream in the course of a season. On a warm spring day I can walk along the bank and select any one of twenty or thirty feeding fish to work over. Some of these sunfish will go eight or nine inches in length, and needless to say, there's a great deal of fun in taking them on. These sunfish are in the seven-to-ten-year group, indicating considerable caution in their attitude toward taking a bait. Except in highly productive lakes, panfish as a rule are surprisingly old by the time they reach a fighting size.

Bluegills get to be very crafty fish. Did you ever watch a school of them in the water? A trout or pike would rush away the instant an angler came in view, but not the bluegill. Most people think the fish have bad eyesight because they go about their business in plain view, but actually they can read the label on your rod. You're just getting the cold shoulder. If you become a nuisance the school will drift away, but otherwise the bluegill will keep one eye on you and one eye on his lunch. This usually frustrates the beginner, who may spend hours flipping baits at them, under the delusion that he hasn't been spotted. No, the bluegill is too cunning for the over-anxious intruder.

It took me ten years to catch a 2-pound bluegill, even though I had fished some of our best panfish waters. Twenty-mile long Claytor Lake in southwest Virginia is really an impoundment of the New River. When Bill Freeman invited me along that morning, his plan was to plug a few miles of shore line for bass. We did remarkably well for that matter, taking smallmouths, spotted bass, and a few largemouths—this alone was worth the trip. I had strung up a light fly rod, with a fat wool-bodied palmer as insurance against an empty stringer, but as things turned out, I never put my plugging rod down all morning.

About noon we started into a rocky cove for lunch, and a school of bluegills cruised across our bow. Bill played his bait in front of them, but the fish moved further up the cove to a cropping of boulders. Bluegills have magnetic quality for me, so a few minutes later I was crawling over the rock, waving a fly at them. The first cast fell short, but the second cast brought one rushing to his doom. This school was so innocent that they came up again and again, and finally a bluegill that looked as big as a dinner plate bolted from the bottom, taking the fly in a neat turn. It was a play that would shame any trout of equal weight, and I was glad when he finally quit.

I do more panfishing now than in years past. The word "panfish" more or less lumps a number of species under one label, yet they have as many distinct characteristics as the whole panoply of gamefish. Some thrive in acid waters, others in alkaline waters, and their individual habitats vary from weedy pond bottoms to tidal creeks and clear mountain streams. If there is a common denominator it's that productive panfishing is subject to as much variety as we have species of fish to confuse us. The methods that are successful on one species may not produce a strike from another and this is further complicated by season and geography. The redbreast sunfish, for example, is normally a piscivorous species and most readily caught on minnows or fish imitating lures such as spinners and streamer flies. By contrast, the redear sunfish feeds primarily on mollusks and crustaceans; minnows and insects are very minor items of its diet. The redear crushes snails between specialized grinding teeth, much in the fashion of a bonefish. During their

bedding season it's fairly easy to fill a stringer with
"shellcrackers," but at other times it's like looking for a
needle in a haystack. Redears are very wary of artificial
lures (unlike most other sunfish), yet they will go on a
rare feeding spree and hit flies and bugs, making the angler
believe that he has discovered a surefire pattern. The fact is
that they are the most difficult panfish to catch on an
everyday basis.

When bluegills are bedding they can be hooked with
anything—even a gumdrop. The fish constantly circles and
defends its nest. About 99 per cent of all the bluegills
caught during this period are dark-colored males who are
protecting the eggs. When you analyze it, this tells us very
little about their feeding habits. If a fair ratio of females are
taken, which is the norm during the rest of the season, then
we get a more balanced picture of effective fishing methods.
The bluegill is dominantly an insect feeder. At times it
eats large amounts of plant material such as algae and
duckweed and only occasionally a small fish or mollusk. In
a number of biological studies made in Wisconsin, Michigan,
Tennessee, and Alabama, for example, midge larvae,
dragonfly and mayfly nymphs, and caddis larvae ranked
as principal foods. One report revealed a remarkable
selectivity, with volumetric consumption of midge larvae
at 100 per cent, despite the presence of other forage. This
doesn't mean that you won't catch the odd bluegill on a
popping bug, but to some extent it explains some of those
awfully blank days when nothing seems to work.

INDEX